AA POCKET GUIDE

CANARY ISLANDS

Written by Adam Hopkins and
Gabrielle MacPhedran
Verified by Paul Murphy
Peace and Quiet section
by Paul Sterry

© Automobile Association
Developments Limited 1996
First published 1991 as *Essential
Canary Islands*
Reprinted 1993 (twice)
Revised second edition 1994
Reprinted 1994; 1995 (twice)
Revised third edition 1996
Reprinted March 1998
Reprinted as *Pocket Guide Canary
Islands* Feb 1999; May 1999
Reprinted 2000
Reprinted 2002, 2003

Maps © Automobile Association
Developments Limited 1996, 2000

Published and distributed in the
United Kingdom by AA Publishing,
which is a trading name of
Automobile Association
Developments Limited, whose
registered office is Millstream,
Maidenhead Road, Windsor,
Berkshire, SL4 5GD.
Registered number 1878835.

A CIP catalogue record for this book
is available from the British Library.

ISBN 0 7495 2114 7

Automobile Association
Developments Limited retains the
copyright in the original edition
© 1991 and in all subsequent editions,
reprints and amendments

A01577

Colour separation: BTB Colour
Reproduction Ltd, Whitchurch,
Hampshire

Printed by: Printer Trento srl, Italy

Front cover picture: *Playa Blanca,
Lanzarote* (AA Photo Library –
S L Day)

Contents

This book employs a simple
rating system to help choose
which places to visit:

✓	'top ten'

♦♦♦ do not miss
♦♦   see if you can
♦   worth seeing if you
     have time

INTRODUCTION

The Canary Islands lie not far north of the Tropic of Cancer and close to the shoulder of Saharan Africa. They are the nearest places to Northern Europe with real hope of winter sun. The summer climate is milder than one might expect, hot but pleasurable. It is this outstanding climate, potentially offering a year-round season, which has been the Canaries' fortune and misfortune. Booming tourism in the 1960s and 1970s led to the construction of colossal and still-growing resorts in the two largest islands, Tenerife and Gran Canaria (the latter also known under the name of its capital city, Las Palmas). These two destinations are certainly familiar to all readers of holiday advertisements, their resorts much loved by some and abominated by others. In recent years the smaller, volcanic island of Lanzarote has joined the tourist listings in a big way.

The pity of it is that those who do not know the Canaries believe the mass holiday phenomenon is the whole story. In fact, the seven Canary

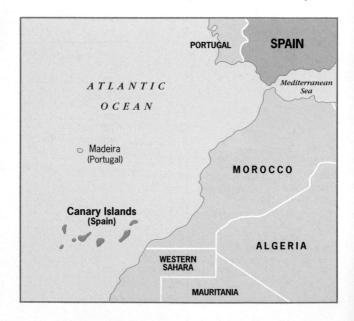

Prickly pears were first grown in the Canaries as an important crop, but many now grow semi-wild

Islands and their lesser islets offer astonishing physical variety and scenes of the greatest natural beauty, by turns savage and peaceful, and ranging in vegetation from the lushest greenery to outright desert. Even the islands with the biggest number of visitors retain large tracts of untroubled countryside, sometimes given over to vines, bananas and other tropical produce but even more often wild and mountainous. Some of the islands, unbelievably, are virtually untouched by tourism.

Basically, there are two groups. The eastern islands are Gran Canaria, Lanzarote and Fuerteventura lying close to Africa. Then there are the western islands, Tenerife, La Gomera, El Hierro and La Palma (not to be confused with Las Palmas), riding a little further out into the Atlantic Ocean.

Of the first group, Gran Canaria/Las Palmas has on its southern side one of the biggest seaside resorts in the whole of Spain and her possessions – on a par with Benidorm and Torremolinos. This is both a plus and a minus. Lanzarote, now becoming very popular, is a moonscape of craters and volcanoes, one at least – Timanfaya, – still impressively active. Fuerteventura is a desert island, barren and strange and ringed by brilliant beaches.

Of the outer group, Tenerife is the largest. In fact, it is considerably the biggest of all the Canary Islands. The individual resorts, however, are just a little smaller than those on Las Palmas, though they do exist on both the north and south sides of the island. In the middle stands Spain's highest mountain, the vast volcanic cone of Teide, surrounded on all sides by spectacular landscapes. Tenerife is certainly an island of extremes. But it is the tiny islands out to the west again which are perhaps the most extraordinary, true gems of the Atlantic Ocean. La Palma and La Gomera in particular remain to this day genuinely unspoilt. Both are strange and lofty, astonishingly beautiful, not so wonderful for swimming but ideal for lovers of nature, for walkers and for those in search of unhassled relaxation.

The fact is that the Canaries offer an island for every taste, whether the preference is for solitude or cheerful, gregarious holidays. The trick is to think carefully in advance and choose the island most suitable for you. The result may very well be enchantment.

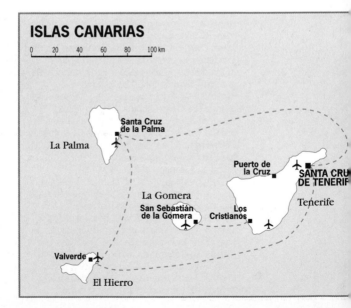

ISLAS CANARIAS

0   20   40   60   80   100 km

La Palma

Santa Cruz
de la Palma

La Gomera
San Sebastián
de la Gomera

Los
Cristianos

Puerto de
la Cruz

SANTA CRUZ
DE TENERIFE

Tenerife

Valverde

El Hierro

BACKGROUND

The Canaries have been known to Europe,
albeit vaguely, since the dawn of recorded
history. The Greeks called them the Fortunate
Islands and romantically inclined historians
have linked them with the lost continent of
Atlantis. From long before recorded history,
however, and right up to the 15th century AD,
they were inhabited by the Guanches, a
simple, vigorous people of unknown origins.
Conquest by Spain devastated their
communities and civilisation. Now the islands
are truly Spanish, peopled by Spaniards
intermingled with the last remnants of the
Guanches. They are administered, in two
provinces, as if they were part of mainland
Spain. Like other large regions of Spain, they
now enjoy a degree of local autonomy.

In the early days of Spanish rule, the agriculture
of the islands produced enough food for the
limited population. Later, the population outgrew
the resources. From that time onwards, the most
appropriate name might well have been the

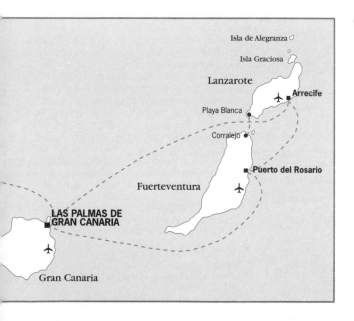

BACKGROUND

Gran Canaria is famous for its beaches, but in the north it has high green hills like these, near Agaete

Unfortunate Islands. Grinding poverty led to mass emigration, mainly to Latin America. The period of the Civil War and Franco dictatorship – 1936–75 – was harder still for the islands, largely because of neglect from Madrid. Now tourism has brightened prospects immeasurably and the new democratic government of Spain has been careful to put the Canary Islands back on the national map.

Yet even now there are problems, not least in tourism. Overbuilding in the resorts of Tenerife and Gran Canaria, and potential overbuilding in Lanzarote, threatens the very market it was intended to serve. Meanwhile the reduction in the cost of long-haul holidays means that winter sun can be found in more exotic destinations at comparable and sometimes lower prices. The long term result may in the end be beneficial for the Canaries. With growing competition for tourists and the changing demands of the market, the quality of the environment becomes a higher priority. And in the end that must serve the best interests of the islander as well as the tourist.

Canarian Balconies
These open-sided balconies of Canarian pine are a delightful and distinctive feature of island architecture. They have carved wooden panels up to knee height or a little higher. The panels are surmounted by prettily-turned balusters. Uprights at the corners support tiled roofs over each balcony.

THE WESTERN ISLANDS: TENERIFE, LA GOMERA, EL HIERRO AND LA PALMA

TENERIFE

General Information

Size: 794 square miles (2,057sq km). Approx 26 miles (42km) east to west across the centre, 27½ miles (44km) north to south, but spreading to 50 miles (80km) along its north coast. Highest point: Pico del Teide, Mt Teide, 12,199 feet (3,710m). Population: 650,000.

The volcanic cone of Teide, centrepiece of Tenerife and highest mountain in all of Spain and her possessions, soars out of the Atlantic to stand as the great symbol of the Canary Islands. Teide was actually in eruption as the tiny ships of Columbus sailed past in 1492 on their voyage of discovery. Tenerife has been giving a welcome to visitors from northern Europe since the 19th century, when those under doctor's orders or simply in search of winter warmth would sometimes visit here instead of the French Riviera.
Then, as now, the essential factor was the island's climate. The north coast, always temperate but often cloudy, was the original point of attraction, in part because of its magnificent plants and trees and general sense of plenty. This coast retains its popularity, particularly among the older generation, and today it draws in visitors from the whole of Europe. But as in a number of the Canary Islands, the south of Tenerife has a different microclimate from the north, being altogether hotter and drier. Over recent years, this has proved an irresistible attraction to younger visitors. Huge, entirely modern resorts, posing considerable environmental problems, now boom away on a coast that until just recently had little to show for itself other than harsh black rock and a handful of tiny beaches. This is still not the best place for sea bathing despite the introduction of some artificial beaches, but blue skies, hotels and apartments, shops,

Los Roques de García, one of the bizarre features of Tenerife's volcanic national park

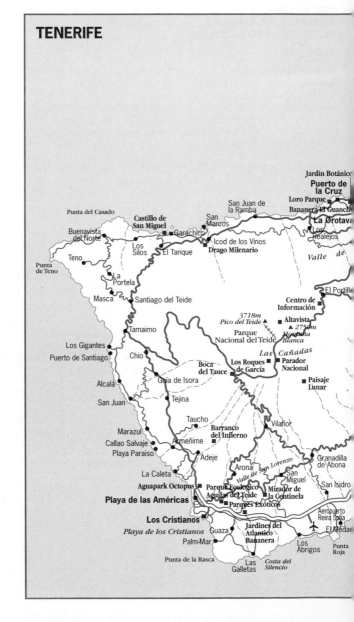

TENERIFE

Jardín Botánico
Puerto de la Cruz
Loro Parque
Banana El Guanch
La Orotava
Los Realejos

San Juan de la Ramba
San Marcos
Punta del Casado
Castillo de San Miguel
Garachico
Buenavista del Norte
Los Silos
El Tanque
Icod de los Vinos
Drago Milenario
Valle de

Teno
La Portela
Punta de Teno
Masca
Santiago del Teide
El Portill
Centro de Información

3718m
Pico del Teide ▲
Tamaimo
Altavista
▲ *2750m*
Montaña Blanca
Parque Nacional del Teide
Las Cañadas

Los Gigantes
Puerto de Santiago
Chio
Boca del Tauce
Los Roques de García
Parador Nacional

Alcalá
Guía de Isora
■ **Paisaje Lunar**

San Juan
Tejina

Taucho
Barranco del Infierno
Vilaflor

Marazul
Armeñime
Callao Salvaje
Playa Paraiso
Adeje
Arona
Valle de San Lorenzo
Granadilla de Abona
San Miguel
San Isidro

La Caleta
Aguapark Octopus
Parque Ecológico
Águilas del Teide
Mirador de la Centinela
Aeropuerto Reina Sofía
El Médar
Playa de las Américas
■ **Parques Exóticos**

Los Cristianos
Playa de los Cristianos
Guaza
Jardines del Atlántico Bananera
Los Abrigos
Punta Roja
Palm-Mar
Punta de la Rasca
Las Galletas
Costa del Silencio

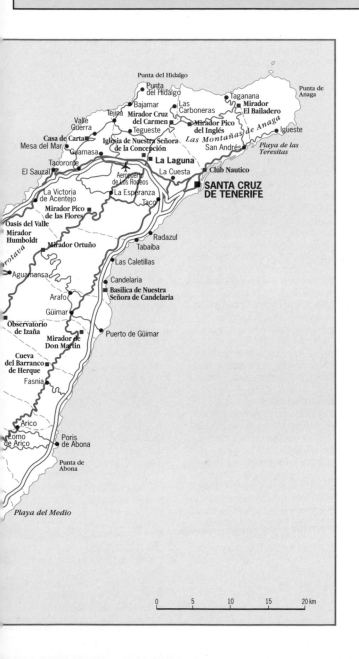

restaurants and discos combine to spread a holiday atmosphere. The other great attraction of Tenerife is the large number of possible excursions to all kinds of entertainments and places of special historic, architectural and scenic interest. In this respect, it is easily the richest of the Canary Islands.

The spectacular volcanic landscape around Teide is a national park: Parque Nacional del Teide. The trade winds make their first contact with the island at the northeast corner, and the higher peaks here are often enveloped in cloud. This rolls on towards the centre of the islands so that the cone of Teide frequently has a ring of cloud around its middle, leaving the land below clear but sometimes in shadow. Meanwhile the mountain, often snow-covered, rises grandly above its cloudy ring. A fair amount of rain falls in the northwest in particular and along the north coast in general.

Island History

The Spanish nobleman Alonso Fernández de Lugo overcame Guanche resistance during bitter fighting from 1494 to 1496, and the local population appears to have been slowly absorbed. The island was attacked several times, always unsuccessfully, by the British, on the last occasion (1797) by Nelson (see Santa Cruz, **What to See**, below). In 1927, when the Canaries were divided into two provinces, the city of Santa Cruz became capital of the province containing all the western islands – La Palma, El Hierro and La Gomera, as well as Tenerife

itself. In 1936, General Francisco Franco met here with fellow army officers to plan the *coup* attempt which led to Spain's bitter civil war.

RESORTS

BAJAMAR

One of the oldest resorts of Tenerife, Bajamar makes a sharp contrast to the glitzier newcomers on the south coast. Backed by dramatic country-side, it is a quieter and less crowded holiday environment. There is a black sand beach and a seashore lido.

EL MÉDANO

This small but burgeoning resort, close to the airport, boasts the best of the southern beaches. It is popular with British visitors and strong gusts make it a great favourite for experienced windsurfers, particularly in July when the World Cup is held here.

LA CALETA

La Caleta and its area, north of Playa de las Américas, is marked by massive individual buildings. This coast holds out little by way of charm or tolerable beaches.

LAS GALLETAS

Entirely different in character from Los Cristianos just along the coast, Las Galletas consists of low-rise developments, running well back from the sea and set among considerable

Los Cristianos has a Mediterranean atmosphere, and is part of a popular resort complex

amounts of space, often with fine gardens. Sea swimming is poor but there are plenty of pools to compensate. A Belgian-inspired development named Ten-Bel overshadows the rest. There is a fairly drab little local town and a small harbour.

LOS CRISTIANOS
Today Los Cristianos has virtually joined itself on to the end of Playa de las Américas to form the largest resort complex on Tenerife, in size second only to the Maspalomas/Playa del Inglés holiday conurbation on Gran Canaria. Most summer visitors are British, with strong competition from Germans and Scandinavians in winter. The town is a concrete jungle, with many brand new apartment complexes of large, not to say staggering dimensions. But whatever it looks like, many visitors appreciate the modern facilities. The kernel is a non-descript nucleus of older town clustered around a harbour which offers shelter for yachts and fishing boats and serves as the starting point for ferry and hydrofoil to the neighbouring island of La Gomera. The beach is right beside the harbour, virtually part of it, lively but far too small for the needs of the many holiday-makers. Visitors often opt instead for apartment or hotel swimming pools.

LOS GIGANTES/PUERTO DE SANTIAGO
This little resort, growing quite fast thanks to rapid development of time-share apartments, is exceptional for just one reason. It

THE WESTERN ISLANDS – TENERIFE

*The massive cliffs known as
Los Gigantes drop almost sheer
from 1,640 feet (500m)*

offers a close-up view of the cliffs
of Los Gigantes, rising vertically
out of the water opposite and
reaching straight up into the sky.
Boats proceeding along the base
of this prodigious cliffscape look
ridiculously, frighteningly small.

PUERTO DE LA CRUZ
Puerto – as it is abbreviated to –
is the most established and the
most attractive of the major
resorts on Tenerife. Though
marred by one or two
excessively large buildings,
Puerto has a special atmosphere
because of its old town.
There are numerous hotels at
either end of the old town, a
newly created black-sand beach
and exceptional opportunities for
pool and poolside relaxation.
Cloudier, cooler and more
cosmopolitan than the south, it is
generally preferred by the older
generation of British visitors,
though there are plenty of young
people here too.

◆◆
PLAYA DE LAS AMÉRICAS
This exceptionally busy resort,
with almost a gold-rush
atmosphere, has grown up since
the 1970s without any kind of
older nucleus. It lies on the flat,
consisting of a busy main street
of bars, restaurants and shops,
pulsing with neon and flowing
with scantily dressed holiday-
makers. This 'main drag' runs
one block back from the shore,
while the young town grows
inland. At the southwest end of
the strip, there is a quieter zone
of hotels, and at the north end a
mixed zone of hotels and
apartment blocks. Almost all the
hotels are very large indeed. The
shoreline is in places composed
of blackish rock, in other parts of
artificial sandy beach contained
by stone breakwaters. The

beaches become exceedingly crowded, with waterskiing, jet-skiing, parascending and other watersports just offshore. By night, the atmosphere can sometimes cross the border into rowdiness, particularly in the area of the Verónicas, a series of little commercial centres housing mainly bars, Mostly, though, good-hearted liveliness prevails.

SANTA CRUZ DE TENERIFE

The major Spanish port of Santa Cruz became the capital of all the islands in 1723, replacing La Laguna 6 miles (10km) away. In 1927 it was demoted somewhat, becoming capital simply of the province of Tenerife, which includes all four western islands. The city now alternates with Las Palmas in Gran Canaria, capital of the eastern islands, as seat of the recently appointed government of the Canary Islands. Santa Cruz occupies an arc of land between the sea and the base of dramatic, forbidding mountains piled up very steep behind. Moving inland from sea to mountain, the various zones of which the town is made are clearly visible. The first consists of extensive port installations, able to handle everything from yachts to ocean-going trawlers to cruise ships and large tankers. Watching the shipping is one of the pleasures of the town. Next comes a promenade, with the Plaza de España, emotional and touristic hub of town, at its southern end. The main shopping streets lead inland from the Plaza de España. The shopping district occupies only a

small area, and quickly gives way to a turn-of-century residential district with handsome villas.

WHAT TO SEE IN SANTA CRUZ

FRANCO MONUMENT
At the opposite end of the front from the Plaza de España and its memorial to the Civil War dead, there stands a highly romanticised monument to General Franco, victor in that war and absolute dictator of Spain from 1939 until his death in 1975.

IGLESIA DE NUESTRA SEÑORA DE LA CONCEPCIÓN
Plaza de la Iglesia
This fine 16th-century church, its tower capped by an octagonal belfry, and the cluster of buildings attached to it, are all that remain of the oldest part of Santa Cruz, destroyed in living memory and much lamented. Within are Lord Nelson's captured battle flag, the tomb of General Gutierrez, defender of of Santa Cruz, and the cross carried by the island's 15th-century Spanish conquerors.

MERCADO DE NUESTRA SEÑORA DE AFRICA
The Market of Our Lady of Africa is a surprisingly small but purpose-built walled enclosure and basement full of shops and stalls, with a good deal of animation. It is entered via an arched gateway close to the dry watercourse which cuts through the southern side of the town centre.

MUSEO ARQUEOLÓGICO
Calle Fuentes Morales (the main entrance is on the Iglesia de NS de la Concepción side)
This extraordinary museum, situated in a most attractive former hospital with an inner gallaried courtyard, deals seriously but accessibly with the archaeology, anthropology and ethnography of the Canaries, as well as the islands' natural history. It contains pottery, clothing of skins, spears without barbs skeletons and a mass of skulls and jawbones packed tight inside each other. Most fascinating of all are the Guanche mummies.
Open: Tuesday to Sunday 10.00–20.00hrs (last tickets sold at 19.00).
Closed: Monday.

◆

MUSEO MILITAR (MILITARY MUSEUM)
Calle San Isidro 2
El Tigre ('the Tiger'), the cannon whose blast removed Lord Nelson's arm, is the most notable exhibit in this collection of hardware and regalia.
Open: Tuesday to Sunday 10.00–13.30hrs.
Closed: Monday.

◆◆

MUSEO MUNICIPAL DE BELLAS ARTES
Calle José Murphy 4
The Fine Arts Museum has ship models, coins, arms and armour – but best are the paintings which include some Flemish and Spanish masters and more recent Canarian works. The museum is in the Plaza del Principe, a pleasing square with trees and bandstand. Note in one corner the elaborate decoration of the Círculo de Amistad de Enero 1855 (Circle of Friendship of January 1855). Next to the square and museum, though facing on to the street below, the church of San Francisco has barley sugar columns and an elegantly

SANTA CRUZ DE TENERIFE

curvaceous top to its façade.
Open: Monday to Friday
10.00–20.00hrs.
Closed: Sunday.

◆◆
PARQUE SANTIAGO GARCÍA SANABRIA

A relaxed and shady, mature park in the heart of town, with thickets of bamboo, handsome trees and exotic plants and shrubs. In the centre, there is a massive monument with plenty of unclothed torso paying tribute to the local worthy after whom the park is named. There is a floral clock, too, which is much photographed by visitors.

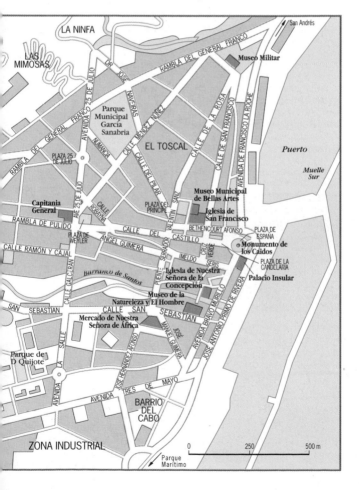

◆◆
PLAZA DE ESPAÑA

This is the hub of Santa Cruz, set on the front between harbour and town. The whole square was formerly the site of the principal Santa Cruz fortification, Castillo San Cristóbal, demolished in 1929. Dominating the square today, is the large grey, Franco-era building of the Palacio Insular, seat of the island council, built in what was called Rationalist style. The solemn Monumento de los Caidos, honours those local people who fell in war, including the Spanish Civil War (1936–9) – Franco's manifesto was broadcast from here. A long reflecting mirror is set into each side in the shape of a sword.

Civil War monument in the Plaza de España, Santa Cruz

◆
PLAZA DE LA CANDELARIA

A pedestrianised rectangle lying just on the town side of the Plaza de España and giving access to the Calle del Castillo (see **Shopping**, below). The seaward side of the square is adorned with an important monument, the late 18th-century Triumph of the Virgin of Candelaria, by the Italian Antonio Canova, celebrating the Spanish conquest of the Guanches. The Virgin is on top of a tall column, with four conquered Guanche chieftains beneath her.

◆
PLAZA 25 DE JULIO

This normally overlooked square, or rather circle, has a fine ceramic pond and set of benches bearing 1920s style advertisements, all created in decorative tiles.

◆◆◆
LAS TERESITAS

San Andrés, 6 miles (10km) northwest of Santa Cruz
Las Teresitas is a crescent of golden sand imported from the Sahara. The sand is held firmly in place by a system of breakwaters. It is easily the best stretch of beach on Tenerife, heavily used in summer by townspeople from Santa Cruz and La Laguna, but deserted in winter. Since foreigners are keen to swim at times when good Canarians stay well-wrapped up indoors, there have been many schemes for tourist development of the land behind Las Teresitas. Debates are acrimonious; the future uncertain.

WHAT TO SEE OUTSIDE SANTA CRUZ

ANAGA MOUNTAINS

These are the extremely steep but not very high mountains (3,360 feet/1,024m) which back the city of Santa Cruz de Tenerife and form a backbone to the island's northeast corner. A road from La Laguna (or Tegueste) follows the most dramatic portions of the range, offering a series of fine lookout points (*miradores*), some back over La Laguna, others out over the precipitous countryside and down to the sea below. Taken in order, these viewpoints are Cruz del Carmen, Pico del Inglés and El Bailadero. It is also possible to climb up from San Andrés, on the coast north of Santa Cruz (in which case the viewpoints will be reached in reverse order). From El Bailadero, a road descends steeply to remote Taganana. Vegetation is surprisingly lush, with 'laurasilva' or laurel forest at medium altitude. It is often misty in this corner of the island: save the route for a clear day.

CALDERA DE LAS CAÑADAS
see **PARQUE NACIONAL DEL TEIDE**

◆◆

CANDELARIA
15 miles (24km) southwest of Santa Cruz
The Basilica de Nuestra Señora de Candelaria, sited towards the south of this growing coastal town, is the island's main place of pilgrimage. Visitors to the church first enter

The basilica of Candelaria is an important place of pilgrimage

a huge open square with, to the left along the sea wall, large pseudo-primitive sculptures of Guanche chieftains.
A very big, modern (1958) church occupies the far side of the square. Within, usually surrounded by wagon-loads of strelitzias, roses and carnations, stands an unremarkable but richly dressed statue of the Virgin. According to legend, a statue of the Virgin was miraculously washed ashore here during the days of the pagan Guanches, and with its presence Candelaria became a shrine for the Spaniards when they later arrived.

The centuries-old dragon tree at Icod de los Vinos, over 52 feet (16m) tall, with a girth of 20 feet (6m)

♦♦
CASA DE CARTA
44 Carretera Tacoronte–Valle Guerra (leave North freeway at Guamasa exit to Valle Guerra intersection and to Boqueron)
The Casa de Carta is an archetypal example of old-fashioned Canarian country architecture. It has been turned into the island's official Ethnographical Museum, partnering the Archaeological Museum in Santa Cruz. Exhibits include weaving and needle-work, traditional costumes and *gofio*-making (*gofio* is a kind of all-purpose flour widely used on the islands).

Open: Tuesday to Saturday 10.00–20.00hrs,
Sunday 10.00–14.00hrs.
Closed: Monday.

♦♦
GARACHICO
This little coastal town offered the best harbour on the north coast up to 1706 when it was rudely filled in by a tide of lava from an eruption above. Several historic buildings survived and together with the rebuilt (but already antique) streets they make this one of the prettiest places in Tenerife, with plenty of wooden Canarian balconies. There is a harbour, too, though more modest than the original. The high hills behind are so steep as to be almost cliffs. Just offshore is the Roque de Garachico, a large black rock, almost an islet.

♦♦♦
ICOD DE LOS VINOS
It's the Drago Milenario (thousand-year-old dragon tree) which makes this small town a compulsory stopping-place – even though no one is quite sure of its true age. And yes, the tree is fantastic, dwarfing the tourist groups which cluster around. Its monstrous trunk is hour-glass shaped, looking as if composed of concrete rivulets (with a little real concrete about its base). An unbelievable number of twisty branches spring out from the top of the trunk and at the end of each is what looks like a fiercely primitive cactus. To one side, above the dragon tree and round an attractive old church, a great number of lesser but still spectacular trees of many species stand on a large terrace.

Above is a little square where the pleasant old buildings have time-worn Canarian balconies.

◆◆◆
LA LAGUNA
Alonso Fernandez de Lugo, conqueror of Tenerife, established La Laguna as his capital in 1496. It has tended recently to spill in all directions, but the old centre remains one of the most pleasant places in Tenerife. It has an air of faded dignity, a selection of old streets and squares with impressive portals and façades, and some outstanding buildings.

Calle de San Agustín
Perhaps the most interesting single street in La Laguna, it leads from the general area of the Concepción church (see below) past the grey stone belfry of the Instituto Cabrera Pinto, the Convent of San Agustín, the baroque Episcopal Palace, the façade of the old university building and the Museu de Historia de Tenerife (see below).

Cathedral
Pink, white and grey, complete with modest dome, the cathedral has a duck pond, often lively with Muscovies, right by its main front. The building, founded in the early 16th century, achieved its current form at the beginning of the 20th century.

Iglesia de Nuestra Señora de la Concepción
One of the finest church buildings on Tenerife, long, low and cream coloured with stone trimmings, and dominated by a handsome tower. Within, note the dark and elaborately carved pulpit and statue of the Virgin, her left breast pierced by a most realistic-looking, shiny sword.

Museu de Historia de Tenerife
This recently opened museum charts the history of the island from the Conquest to the present day with a series of very well-displayed exhibits. The star attraction is the building itself, the Casa de Lercaro, built in 1593.

Plaza del Adelantado
A square with handsome buildings and a real sense of Old Spain. On the corner of the square and the narrow cranny of the Calle Déan Palahi, the convent of Santa Catalina has a notable Canarian balcony (in this case, a gallery) with elaborate wooden lattice work.

◆◆◆
MASCA
Teno, northwest Tenerife
At the heart of the mountainous Teno district, Masca is a must for lovers of dramatic scenery. The narrow road from Tamaimo first climbs up over a small ridge offering notable views of Teide behind and above. Once across the ridge, it descends steeply through tight hairpins, revealing a countryside deeply cleft by ravines. Sharp ridges rise like the backs of dinosaurs to the height of the road. The ancient roofs of the much-visited village lie beneath the road. Looking back, one sees that the ravine positively bristles with rocky out-crops, and glistens with wind-blown palms. The road continues, high and thrilling but generally well guarded, to La Portela.

*This tranquil view over La Orotava
has changed little over the
centuries*

It then follows an easy descent to
Buenavista on the north coast.
(This journey is equally dramatic
the other way round.)

◆◆◆
LA OROTAVA ✓

Valle de la Orotava
Though not far above Puerto de
la Cruz, this town has a firmly
defined character of its own. Its
old centre, still remarkably well
preserved, houses a rich jumble
of mansions, convent and
monastery, pleasing public
places and churches.

Casa de los Balcones
This mansion on the Calle de
San Francisco has been
converted into a museum/shop
of local handicrafts, and makes a
convenient starting point for
exploring the town. It lives up to
its name, which means 'House of
Balconies'. Those outside are
really galleries rather than
balconies, rather too obviously
conserved. Inside, two tiers of
beautiful and elaborate balconies
rise above a pretty, ancient-
feeling courtyard. Just opposite is
another noteworthy mansion used
for the same purposes – La Casa
del Turista, dating from 1590.

Hijuela del Botánico
The name literally means 'Little
Daughter of the Botanic Garden'
– the one in Puerto de la Cruz. It
is a densely packed garden of
trees and shrubs behind the
town hall, with a dragon tree at
the centre.

Hospital of the Holy Trinity
Located almost opposite the
Casa de los Balcones, there is a
doorway immediately below the

main building which leads onto a terrace/balcony offering a view of the beautiful but increasingly built-up Valle de la Orotava. Set into the main door of the hospital (which now cares for mentally handicapped patients) is a revolving wooden drum, open on one side. Unwanted babies were once deposited in the open side of the barrel; one twirl and off they went through the door to care and safety of the nuns within.

Iglesia de Nuestra Señora de la Concepción
A late 18th-century church. To the left of the large alabaster altar (a survivor from an earlier church on the same spot) there is a large screen of the Conception, to the right a grey-painted screen apparently carved from stone. Tap it and you will find that it is wooden. Masses of flowers usually adorn this baroque building, centre of the Corpus Christi flower festival.

Plaza de la Constitución
Yellow cassias bloom in ordered rows around a cream-coloured bandstand in this delectable spot with its fine views towards the coast. At one extreme stands the yellow façade of San Agustín, with Canarian carved doors. From further along the square, a steep garden, rich in strelitzias and flowering shrubs, ascends towards the ornate building of the **Liceo de Taoro**. This is a private club where members doze on plum-coloured sofas in a kind of Victorian time-warp. Exhibitions and recitals are held here and admission to the club is also open to the public.

♦♦♦
PARQUE NACIONAL DEL TEIDE ✓

Mount Teide, huge and impressive as it is, was not the original centre or high-point of the island. This was a yet greater volcanic mountain standing immediately to the south. Millions of years ago, the ancient monster either erupted or collapsed in on itself, leaving a gigantic crater. Mount Teide is no more than a large cone lying on the edge of this crater, which in its way is even more spectacular than Teide itself. The name of the crater is Caldera de las Cañadas. The crater and Mount Teide together make up the Teide National Park.

Getting there
The journey up from the coast is part of the event, and is quite different on either side of the mountain. The climb from the comparatively arid south – via San Isidro, Granadilla and Vilaflor or from Playa de las Américas via Chio – starts in scrubby, ravine-rent country, passes through vineyards and finally sparse pine forest before bringing the visitor over the lip of the crater and down into its awesomely rocky bowl. The Granadilla/Vilaflor road enters via a striking pass, the **Boca de Tauce**. The journey from the north – directly up from Puerto de la Cruz and La Orotava or along the northeast ridge from La Laguna and La Esperanza – leads through well-cultivated farmland, with flowers and patches of sweet corn, then up

through often cloudy, moist green forest, and so across the lip into the crater. Even if Mount Teide appears from below to be blocked off by cloud, the chances are that all will be clear on top.

Caldera de las Cañadas

The crater lies at about 6,200 feet (2,000m). It is 30 miles (48km) in circumference and 10 miles (16km) in diameter, with Teide rising above to the north and the remainder enclosed by high rock walls. In places these rise over 1,550 feet (500m) from the floor of the crater. Sometimes black, sometimes red, this is mostly a wild mass of bare volcanic stone. It lies in huge ridges as if shoved into untidy form by bulldozers. A rib of extravagantly-shaped rocks – **Los Roques de García** – at one point runs across the floor of the crater from Teide towards the outer rim. Near the Boca de Tauce a *mirador* (viewpoint) leads the eye upwards towards a pair of blackened holes on a lesser mountainside – **Las Narices**, the Nostrils, scene of an eruption, at the end of the 18th century.

Teide

This loftiest of Spanish mountains, with views over the whole chain of the Canary Islands, has attracted visitors for hundreds of years; in 1910 the astronomer Jean Mascourt took the first photographs of Halley's Comet from the mountain. The ascent on foot traditionally took two days, commencing from La Orotava and with a stop at Altavista, site of the present mountain refuge. Today most visitors drive, then make the

Caldera de Las Cañadas, the crater of a once-huge volcano

final part of the ascent by cable car. This climbs from 7,730 feet (2,356m) to 11,670 feet (3,555m) in just eight minutes, leaving a further 524 feet (160m) to walk. A permit is needed to complete the final section, available from Park Office in Santa Cruz. Note: the car does not operate when it is very windy – which is common in winter.

National Park Information

On entry to the park in the northwest, at **El Portillo** (close

to the junction of the roads from La Orotava and La Laguna) there is a visitors' centre offering information on guided and/or signposted walks and more ambitious hikes.

◆◆◆
PUERTO DE LA CRUZ ✓

The attractive old town of Puerto de la Cruz is clustered round the former harbour, or *puerto* and a lively square, Plaza del Charco. All the town's historic sights are in this area, with other interesting spots to visit within a couple of miles (3–4km). Established a century ago as a holiday resort, Puerto retains its identity and old-world charm.

Avenida de Colón
A promenade on the northeast side of the town, where the sea-walls provide often-spectacular displays of breaking surf. The Avenida de Colón (Columbus) adjoins the Lido Martiánez (see below) and the pebbly beach of Playa Martiánez, which is the starting point of many free bus services to local entertainments within Puerto de la Cruz.

Bananera El Guanche

Just over a mile (2km) from town, on the road to La Orotava, the Bananera is a great family day out which explains all about the banana. It shows an informative video every 20 minutes and offers a chance to wander in a working banana plantation. Free bus from Playa Martiánez.
Open: daily, 09.00–18.00hrs.

Capilla de San Telmo

A simple but very pleasing whitewashed chapel on the front, with a florally painted, Canarian-style altar screen.

Casino Taoro

This large and rather stately ex-hotel above the town, floodlit at night, plies its business as a casino every day of the year. Visitors must be over 18 and carry passports. Free taxi from town. Entrance fee.

Iglesia de la Peña de Francia

With its panelled wooden ceiling, ceramic plaques on the walls and its setting in a pleasant tree-lined square, the principal church of Puerto de la Cruz is pure Canarian in feeling. Sculptures by Luján Pérez, famous local 18th-century artist.

Jardín Botánico/Jardín de Aclimatación

Calle Retama, off Carretera del Botánico
The founder and first director of the Botanical/Acclimatisation Garden was the aptly named Marques de Villanueva del Prado (1788–1832, Prado meaning meadow). The aim was to acclimatise plants and trees to the Canarian climate, then move them on to the Spanish mainland. The plants

Lido Martiánez offers palm-shaded sunbathing alongside blue lagoons

and trees (as also orchids in the orchid house) have done almost excessively well, though few have made the final transfer to Spain.
Open: daily, 09.00–17.00hrs.
Bus along C. del Botánico.

Lido Martiánez
The noted Lanzarote architect César Manrique designed this splendid lido in 1969 in order to give holiday-makers a desirable bathing area. An ample site on the sea front, effectively a promontory backed by the earliest cluster of tourist hotels, has been dramatically fashioned into an area of pools and poolside pleasure. White walls top black volcanic rock, palms nod over light blue lagoons, a large and lumpy rock suddenly reveals itself as the most profuse of fountains while all around, outside, the Atlantic swells and surges.
Open: daily, 09.00–18.00hrs.

Loro Parque
just over 1.5 mile (3km) west from the centre
This Florida-style bird, wildlife and dolphin park claims the world's largest collection of parrots. The birds are paired off in large cages, with displays illustrating the continents where they originated. The well-kept gardens, including a fine show of orchids, are also a pleasure. Sea lions, sharks and dolphins all make this the island's most popular tourist stop. In place is a substantial breeding programme helping to conserve rare species. Free bus from Avenida de Venezuela.
Open: daily, 08.30–17.00hrs.

TEIDE see **PARQUE NACIONAL DEL TEIDE**

VALLE DE LA OROTAVA
A wide but steep-walled depression running down from underneath Mount Teide to the sea, with marvellous views over the 'valley', Puerto de la Cruz and the north coast behind it. Lovely walking country; maps of footpaths are available at tourist information offices.

Accommodation
Los Gigantes/Puerto de Santiago
Barceló Santiago, 4-star (tel: 86 09 12), on rocky, built-up headland, with stunning views of Los Gigantes cliffs. Atmospheric, with good food and rooms.

Playa de las Américas
Bitácora, 4-star (tel: 79 15 40),spacious heated swimming pool and lawn. **Gran Tinerfe**, 4-star (tel: 79 12 00), good views and position.
Vulcano, 4-star (tel: 79 20 35), impressive balconied court, full of palms and dripping greenery from aloft. Pool. Special rooms and facilities for disabled guests.

Puerto de la Cruz
Hotel Botánico, Avenida Richard J Yeoward 1, 5-star (tel: 38 14 00). Magnificent tropical gardens, quiet and comfortable.

Santa Cruz
Mencey Hotel, José Naveiras 38, 5-star (tel: 27 67 00). This spacious hotel, with gleaming marble floors and romantic paintings, is built round patios with Canarian balconies. Pool.

Children
Playa de las Américas area
The **Aguapark Octopus** has outdoor water-slides and many other diversions, and is one of the most popular entertainments of Tenerife. Free bus from Playa de las Américas and Los Cristianos.
Open: daily, 09.00–21.00hrs.

The **Parque Exóticos** is situated off the motorway between Los Cristianos and the Reina Sofia airport at Desierto Feliz. The lush garden claims to display the 'largest cactus collection in the world'. Also houses an animal park to amuse youngsters. There is a free shuttle bus from Los Cristianos.
Open: daily, 10.00–18.00hrs.

Puerto de la Cruz area
Loro Parque (see page 27) is a must for all ages, while water babies will love the **Lido Martiánez** pools and fountains (see page 27). Spotting exotic fruits growing on strange trees at the **Bananera El Guanche** (see page 26) may well appeal to older children. You can take a camel or a burro (donkey) 'safari' at **El Tanque** near Garachico and perhaps combine this with seeing the weird and wonderful **Drago Milenerio** ('1,000-year-old dragon tree') near by at Icod de los Vinos (see pages 20–1).

Culture, Entertainment and Nightlife
Exhibitions, concerts and so on tend to flourish most vigorously in the north, particularly in **Santa Cruz**, **Puerto de la Cruz** and **La Laguna**. Rock concerts are sometimes held at the former bullring in Santa Cruz.

Nightclubs and discos are plentiful. **El Coto Up & Down** at the Oro Negro Hotel is one of the best in Puerto. There is a bewildering choice of nightspots in the south, particularly in Playa de las Américas. The **Palace** at San Eugenio stages Spanish, and international extravaganzas and the Medieval Night at the mock **Castillo San Migel** is hugely popular. For great rhythm 'n' blues head for **Alabama's**, on the road to Granadilla and for the best discos try **Melody** or **Trauma** or (as things change so quickly) simply ask around. To gamble the night away, make for the grand, old **Casino Taoro** in Puerto de la Cruz or the **Casino de las Americas**.

Restaurants
Look out for roadside stalls, particularly on the north coast. These may sell local wines, chestnuts roasted in ashes, and hot, salt sardines.

Adeje
The Chicken Shack in Adeje, up above Playa de las Américas, serves, amongst other things, chicken marinated in mojo sauce and then deep fried, an interesting taste halfway between Delhi and Kentucky.

Agua García
This village draws large crowds of Tenerifeans for Sunday lunch, the sure test of local quality. (Leave the Santa Cruz/Puerto de la Cruz motorway at Tacoronte and travel a short distance inland). Try **El Junquito** or **El Bosque** (simple and hearty, with meat, salad and wine) or **La Florida**, specialising in pork.

La Cuesta de la Villa

High marks for two restaurants neighbouring one another in La Cuesta de la Villa, a village with fine views over Puerto de la Cruz and the Orotava valley. **El Lagar** (tel: 30 08 75) is good quality international, **Los Corales** (tel: 30 02 49) an elegant fish restaurant. Both are expensive.

Garachico

The **Isla Baja** (83 00 08) restaurant surrounds the courtyard of an old house opposite the castle, and specialises in fish. Dining room first floor; downstairs is a lively model of the 1706 eruption.

Los Abrigos

The semi-circular front of this village on a rocky bay not far from Reina Sofia airport is composed almost entirely of fish restaurants. It has a cheerful and lively atmosphere, and is unquestionably the fish-dish centre of the south.

Playa de las Américas

At the top end of the scale, try the **Restaurante Casa Vasca**, situated in the patio of the Compostela Beach Hotel, where the Basque landlord/chef offers Basque dishes. The **Banana Garden**, beside the Palm Beach complex, serves good Mexican and international food. Banana trees and parrots provide colour. There is live music nightly and flamenco shows at weekends. **Bornajo**, on the main street, is middle range; queues form for tasty grills. **El Gomero**, near the edge of town and owned by a Gomeran, offers cheap, hearty food.

Carnations for sale in the flower market, Santa Cruz

Puerto de la Cruz

The **Casa Miranda**, a Canarian mansion on the front near the town hall, is named after its former owners, a Tenerife family whose descendants played a part in the liberation of Latin America. The old mansion is well restored and the dining room is delightful, although it is on the expensive side. Take a five-minute taxi ride out of town in the direction of the Botanical Gardens to **Casa Lala** for cheaper but no less delicious Canarian food. Fish and steaks feature strongly on a small but excellent menu. **Los Gemelos**, just behind the Plaza Charco in the old town, is recommended for good local cooking and·a pleasant atmosphere.

Shopping

Santa Cruz is Tenerife's top shopping centre, despite the arrival of high quality, expensive furs in Puerto de la Cruz and the multitudinous perfume and liquor stores of Playa de las Américas. Most tour companies offer special excursions to Santa Cruz from the resorts, allowing visitors to browse among the Indian-style and often Indian-owned bazaars selling mainly electronic goods. There are some notable handicraft establishments and jewellers. The main shopping area is round the **Plaza de la Candelaria,** including the Calle Castillo (running up from the Plaza de la Candelaria), and Bethencourt Alfonso, running parallel two streets to the northeast. For electronic goods, videos, cameras etc, the main emporium is **Maya**, in a side street off the Plaza de la Candelaria. Good and patient service, no bargaining (as distinct from other bazaar-type shops). Leading handicraft establishments are the excellent **Artespaña**, top right hand corner of Candelaria, and, rather less selective in its stock, the **Casa de los Balcones** on left at entrance to the square from Plaza de España. For **pearls**, try **El Templo** in Béthencourt Alfonso. There are good boutiques in the **Calle Viera y Clavijo** and in the **Rambla de General Franco** near the Hotel Mencey. Cheap **leather goods** are sold near the **Mercado de Nuestra Señora de Africa** and on Sunday mornings there is a *rastro* or **flea market** running along the harbour front from the Club Nautico.

In **Garachico**, **local lace** is on sale in the Centro de Artesanía, opposite the castle, together with other **handicraft items**. There is a handicraft market here on the first Sunday of each month. **La Orotava** has two busy centres for the sale of Canarian handicrafts – **La Casa de los Balcones** and **La Casa del Turista** opposite, both in the Calle San Francisco.

Special Events

Locals claim that the **Santa Cruz Carnival** (February/March) is second only to that of Rio de Janeiro (they make the same claim in Las Palmas, though). Certainly there is lots of fun and little sleep. At **Corpus Christi** (June) **La Orotava** is famous for its flowers. Carpets of petals and intricate patterns in multi-coloured sand offer a brief, extravagant brilliance. There are many smaller scale local festivals throughout the island, at almost all times of year.

Sport

Already developing quickly on Tenerife, **golf** seems likely to become a major attraction for the future, just as it is in Gran Canaria. The main courses are the Real Golf Club de Tenerife at La Laguna, the Amaralla Golf and Country Club and Golf del Sur (Playa de las Américas area). In the same area there is **go-karting** at the Karting Club Tenerife and at Karting Las Américas (free bus to the latter from Playa de las Américas). Real Club Náutico, Santa Cruz de Tenerife, is for **yachts** and **motorboating**, with other facilities such as **tennis**.

LA GOMERA

General Information
Size: 146 square miles (378sq km). 14½ miles (23km) north to south and 15½ miles (25km) east to west.
Highest point: 4,878 feet (1,487m).
Population: 20,000.

Considering its proximity to touristy Tenerife, La Gomera is remarkably unspoiled. It is extraordinarily high in relation to its small land surface, ranking almost with La Palma in this respect; and it is notable for the 'laurasilva' or laurel forest covering its upper surfaces. The Gomerans are a frank and friendly people, inhabiting one of the most splendid and beautiful of the Canary Islands.
In shape, La Gomera is like a very tall cake from which alternate slices have been cut, sometimes slightly off centre. These missing slices are thrillingly deep ravines; to get from one place to another, you are always wiggling up from sea level and over the centre of the island, then descending into another of the ravines. On top of the cake and in places running down the sides, La Gomera has its icing of laurasilva forests. The collision of trade winds and the Gomera mountains produces mist and cloud, drizzle and downpour on the heights, and it is this which makes the forest grow so abundantly. Most of the high centre is a national park – the Parque Nacional de Garajonay. Around the base of the island, more often than not,

A typical contrast of wild cacti and cultivated farmland in the spectacular Valle Gran Rey

the sun shines brilliantly – on comparatively infertile, stony ground in the south, and on vines, bananas, palms, tomatoes and tropical fruit in the valleys of the north.

El Silbo

The most extraordinary feature of La Gomera is *el silbo*, the whistling language invented for communicating across ravines. Immensely powerful sounds are achieved, either by whistling through the fingers or by simple force of lip and air. The whistle is substituted for vocalisation – when you hear it, you almost think you can understand.
It is hard to learn and though some older people still know the 'language', the younger generation often understand but cannot communicate.

Island History

La Gomera is famous chiefly because this was Columbus's final port of call – the last place his foot touched ground – before the historic journey of 1492. He may have returned again in 1493 and in 1498, using La Gomera as a stepping stone for further journeys to the Americas. The island had first been visited on behalf of Spain at the start of the 15th century, by the Norman Jean de Béthencourt, well remembered throughout the Canaries in street names. Hernán Peraza the Elder finally conquered it for Spain in the middle of the century. The tyrannical younger Peraza was murdered by his subjects, leaving his widow, the beautiful and formidable Beatriz de Bobadilla, in control.

The island remained in the possession of the Counts of La Gomera until the 19th century. Its harbour was frequently visited by vessels crossing the Atlantic, and it became as closely involved with the New World as the Old. Economic distress forced many of its inhabitants to emigrate to Latin America. The island suffered particularly under the Franco dictatorship, a time remembered with bitterness. Even today, many Gomerans emigrate, most often now to work in tourism on neighbouring Tenerife.

There are no resorts at all in the sense in which the word applies in Tenerife and Las Palmas, but there is a notable *parador* (see page 114) and one large hotel complex. In 1999 La Gomera's airport opened near Playa de Santiago in the south of the island.

SAN SEBASTIÁN DE LA GOMERA

The island's miniature capital lies behind the bay which Columbus and other early navigators used as an anchorage. Today it is a regular little port, with a quay on the outer side, and a stony beach in front of the town. The ferry leaves two or three times a day for Los Cristianos on Tenerife; hydrofoils make faster and more frequent crossings.

Leaving the long jetty, travellers find themselves in the little tree-filled square of the Plaza de América. All points of interest lie within a few minutes' walk, not to mention the baker, the town hall and island buses.

WHAT TO SEE IN SAN SEBASTIÁN

CASA COLUMBINA
Calle del Medio

Calle del Medio is a little street running inland from the market. Columbus connections are very tenuous but it is at any rate agreeably ancient. Exhibitions concerning La Gomera and its history are occasionally put on here. The house is the focus of annual Columbus celebrations in September. Refer to the tourist office for opening times.

IGLESIA DE LA ASUNCIÓN
Calle del Medio

Some parts of this church may have been in existence when Columbus said his prayers here in 1492 but the bulk of it is 16th century. On entering, it is well worth turning to look back at the handsome dark wood balcony above the doorway. To the left of the (wooden) altar is the Capilla del Pilar, the Chapel of the Pillar, built to commemorate the repulse of an English fleet under Admiral Charles Windham in 1743. A mural, partially lost, shows cannon balls whizzing about. The Puerta del Perdón – Door of Forgiveness – was used by Beatriz de Bobadilla to trick her husband's murderers. She promised pardon to those who passed through it, thus acknowledging their guilt. And then she executed them.

POZO DE COLÓN
The name means Columbus's Well. Just by the vast tree in the

market square there stands a chunkily stone-built, tightly shuttered, single storey house with patio – the former Customs House, now the tourist office. In the centre of the humble patio, a little low well edged with pebbles is honoured as the spot from which Columbus's ships drew water before departing on 6 September 1492. A sign says in Spanish, 'The water from this well baptised America'.

TORRE DEL CONDE

The 'Count's Tower' is a small but stout pink and white brick fort just behind the front. Built in 1447 by Hernán Peraza the Elder, it is the town's only obvious monument and the Canaries' oldest building in continuous use. Beatriz de Bobadilla used it as a refuge after the slaying of her husband, Hernán Peraza the Younger, in 1487, and it is here that the popular imagination brings her together with Columbus.

WHAT TO SEE OUTSIDE SAN SEBASTIÁN

AGULO

A beautiful village perched above the sea with views of Tenerife and Teide, and backed by an amphitheatre of rock, this is a quiet, settled village with cobbled streets. Around a church with a strange, domed roof, the Plaza de Leoncio Bento is a pretty place of pollarded trees and houses with wide wooden doorways. Corniche driving in this part of the island is a delight.

ALOJERA

Far below the main road, but still at some height above the sea, this scattered village occupies an up-and-down patch of land. Below again, after a very steep final descent, there is a modest grey beach where amenities seem likely to expand. The way down from main road to village is unusual: it runs on the outside of the hill rather than inside a ravine. The effect is dramatic.

EL CERCADO

Pottery is produced in this village without benefit of anything so new-fangled as the potter's wheel. Shaped by hand, dabbed in a shiny liquid clay and brushed to take the shine off, it is fired in simple kilns that look like stone-built dog-kennels. The brushwood for the fire is fetched, on foot, from the forest above; the clay is fetched, on foot, from two ravines away. The resulting dishes and jugs look very similar to Guanche pottery on display in the museums of Las Palmas and Santa Cruz de Tenerife.

GARAJONAY see PARQUE NACIONAL DE GARAJONAY

HERMIGUA

A steep descent through a beautiful and fertile valley, where vines grow on bamboo lattices, leads down to several little clusters of village running down a ridge. This is the largest centre of habitation after San Sebastián and a sign, written in Spanish, welcomes

Time seems to have stood still in El Cercado, where pottery is made by traditional methods

visitors to what it claims is 'the best climate in the world'. Visit the Los Telares craft centre to see an old house where girls still weave on ancient looms. Near by is the 16th-century Convento de Santo Domingo, with its Moorish-style ceiling.

LA FORTALEZA
This is a vast rock outcrop to the southwest of the peak of Garajonay, believed to have been held sacred by the Guanches. There are fine views from several lookout points, among them the Mirador of Igualero on the way down to Playa de Santiago.

LOS ÓRGANOS
One of the marvels of the island. Not far from the Playa de Vallehermoso but visible only from the sea, the rocky north-west coast provides an unusual display – a great rock organ composed of thousands of pipes or flutes of basalt packed together as if intentionally. Boat trips from Valle Gran Rey, Playa de Santiago and San Sebastián.

PARQUE NACIONAL DE GARAJONAY
Whether visitors plan to walk the paths and mountain trails of La Gomera or merely to drive the upland roads, the Garajonay national park, covering most of the high interior, will inevitably be one of the main attractions on the island. Its borders follow, fairly exactly, the limits of the ancient 'laurasilva' laurel forests. The dense evergreens of the forest, the spectacular and deeply rent countryside and the tall, eroded rockstacks of Agando, Ojila, Zarcita and Cherelepin help to make time spent in the park memorable. The forest of El Cedro is also specially recommended.

Founded in 1981, the park was declared a World Heritage Site in 1986. There is an information centre at Juego de Bolas (the Game of Bowls) near Las Rosas on the northern side of the island. This provides details of flora and fauna, waymarked trails and other information.

◆◆◆
VALLE GRAN REY

Wild, steep and narrow at the top, a cleft of valley opens beneath the upland village of Arure, offering dramatic viewing points. Two branches of this valley soon run together and broaden downwards into a

Little white houses perch precariously on the steep, terraced slopes of the Valle Gran Rey

single rent in the structure of the island. Terraces climb astonishingly high on either side with groups of houses clustered like swallows' nests. The valley floor is green and fertile, rich in palms and bananas. The main village lies just near the sea, climbing a little upwards. Right down on the coast, to left, there is a harbour and, the right, a beach. Both have settlements behind and both are in the process of slow and shambolic tourist development, despite local protest. The sandy beach offers the best sea swimming on an island which is generally disappointing in this respect.

◆◆
VALLEHERMOSO
Remarkable mainly for featuring in vistas from high above in the Garajonay national park, Vallehermoso lies underneath El Roque Cano, the Dog Rock, a tremendous stump stripped bare by erosion and looking much like a canine tooth. At the Playa de Vallehermoso, the mouth of the ravine is strikingly enclosed in rock, with remnants of old port installations. The near-beach of rocks and pebbles can be extremely inhospitable when seas of any size are running.

Accommodation
Part of the charm of La Comera is its comparative lack of accommodation. Apartments and private rooms are to be found in Valle Gran Rey, there are apartments and a handful of 1- and 2-star hotels in San Sebastián, and that is about it, with two striking exceptions. **The Parador de la Gomera**, 4-star (tel: 87 11 00), is built

high on a bluff of cliff above San Sebastián, looking out over the sea and across the straits to Tenerife. Cleverly constructed round patios, purpose-built in 1973 but agreeably old-world, this is by far the most attractive *parador* (see page 114) in the Canaries and is considered to be one of the best small *paradores* in Spain.

The Hotel Jardin Tecina, Lomada de Tecina, 4-star (tel: 14 58 50), at Playa de Santiago, is constructed on the corner of a cliff above the village. Large numbers of two-storey 'bungalows', one room upstairs and one room down, each reached from winding pathways at front-level, stand in luxuriously flowering gardens.

Restaurants
Hermigua
Just between Hermigua and Agulo, the modest **El Silbo** restaurant offers drinks, meals and a terrace with magnificent views.

Parque Nacional de Garajonay
La Laguna Grande, a rough rock building set in a grassy clearing, offers simple, tasty meals. Used by hikers with rucksacks and all weather gear.

Playa de Santiago
There are several fish restaurants here. The **Junonia**, and **La Quevita**, both near the port, win top ratings from locals. They are small, friendly family-run places, cheap and appetising. The à la carte restaurant of the **Hotel Jardin Tecina**, is one of the island's two top spots for a serious,

The church in Vallehermoso nestles amid subtropical greenery

expensive meal. **San Sebastián,** the restaurant of the *parador* is the other.

Special Events
Columbus Festival, 6 September.

Sport
The **Hotel Jardin Tecina**, Playa de Santiago, has excellent facilities including a **gymnasium**, **swimming**, **tennis** and **squash**. But the main pastime offered by the island is **walking**, more or less strenuously and involving some scrambling, according to the route chosen. Walkers can take themselves along national park trails, and there are Swiss-led hikes (available to all) from the Hotel Jardim Tecina.

EL HIERRO

General Information

Size: 107 square miles (278sq km). 15 miles (24km) from north to south and 17 miles (27km) from east to west.
Highest point: Mount Malpaso 4,925 feet (1,501m).
Population: 7,400.

The smallest and most westerly of the Canary Islands, enclosed by high cliffs and with only a few beaches, El Hierro is undoubtedly the least spoiled of all the islands. Its most loyal admirers return again and again for just that reason. The scenery is as spectacular as any in the Canaries. A high, pine-covered ridge runs east to west, curved in the shape of a boomerang. It is, in fact, one half of the rim of a volcanic crater, with the other half invisible beneath the sea. The inner curve of the boomerang falls steeply on the northern side to form a wide bay or gulf – El Golfo – of the greatest beauty. Its slopes are covered in forests of pine and, above the height of 1,650 feet (500m), often shrouded in mist, so that the pine-needles drip with moisture. In an island so short of water, this is an invaluable asset. Descending, the pines give way to laurel, beech and giant heathers, then to a huge variety of succulent plants and, finally, green pastures divided by dry stone walls. To the south a triangular landmass reaches down towards the sea and here the pastures turn into bleak volcanic hillsides. It can be wet and misty in the north and east

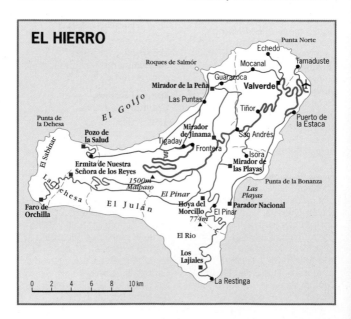

Izique mountain marks the northern end of El Golfo, or 'the gulf', which forms the northern side of boomerang-shaped Hierro

while the sun is shining fit to burst elsewhere on the island. El Hierro is a delight for leisurely exploration and best seen on foot. Tarred roads, however, are well maintained and the rough tracks which have to be negotiated are passable by car without too much difficulty.

Island History

Jean de Béthencourt, Norman adventurer and scourge of the Guanches, landed here in 1405 as representative of the Spanish crown. The local king, Armiche, came down from the mountains to greet the visitors. He and his followers, with most of the male population of the island, were immediately enslaved and sent to Europe. One feels that

El Hierro has never fully recovered. However, the island has one significant claim to fame. Everybody agreed, there was no doubt about it, that the world ended at El Hierro, at least until the discovery of America. Up to 1884, when the mantle fell instead to Greenwich in Britain, zero meridian was placed at the island's most westerly point. It was from El Hierro that Columbus set off in 1493 on his second journey to America. Traditionally, most visitors to El Hierro are Spaniards, and many come from other Canary Islands. The rest are mainly Germans. There are no resorts as such on El Hierro, though tourist accommodation is available at Valverde, Frontera, Tamaduste and La Restinga and, most notably, at the island's *parador*, out on its own in the bay of Las Playas.

VALVERDE

This very modest 'town' (no bigger than a village) is about 4 miles (7km) from the airport and about 6 miles (10km) from Puerto de la Estaca, where the ferry docks. The foundations were laid at the end of the 15th century on the site of an earlier pre-Hispanic settlement. Valverde means Green Valley, a name perhaps more accurately applicable to the view from the town.
All the basic necessities may be found in its two main streets: shops, banks, tourist office, a hotel, bars, a petrol station. But it is the sort of place where you can stand in the dead centre and hear only cocks crowing.

WHAT TO SEE IN VALVERDE

IGLESIA DE LA CONCEPCIÓN

This substantial parish church in the main square was built in the late 18th century on the site of an earlier 16th-century one. In stern grey stone and brilliant white, the broad, triple-aisled front rises to a small tower with a lookout balcony. This is one of many Canarian churches once used as a refuge against pirate attack.

◆
MUSEO INSULAR
Calle Dr Quintero 11
The island's Folk Museum exhibits old domestic implements and tools, and local costume. Opening times are irregular so it is best to enquire at the tourist office.

MUSEO JUAN PEDRÓN
Calle Previsor Magdalena 8
A private house in old Canarian style with a collection of local antiquities. The house and patio are as interesting as the exhibits. Bang on the door and someone may let you in.

WHAT TO SEE OUTSIDE VALVERDE

EL PINAR
These forests of Canary pines are the most characteristic feature of El Hierro, beautiful to drive through, and even better on foot. In either case you can organise your route to pass various *miradores* (lookouts) with breathtaking views of the east coast.
The **Mirador de las Playas** offers a view of the wide curve of Las Playas bay with the Roques Bonanza, a strange rock formation rising straight out of the sea a few feet from the shore. On a clear day you can see La Gomera, La Palma and Tenerife. Further south there is the **Mirador de Tanajora** and in the forest, **Hoya del Morcillo**, a favourite place for Herreños at weekends who come to picnic (barbecue-fuel provided), play football or go walking. There is also a children's playground, toilets, running water and camping facilities.

EL SABINAR
A wood of juniper trees unique to El Hierro (*Juniperus sabina*). The bark of these bizarrely shaped, wind-twisted trees

gives off a pungent aroma and was formerly used as moth repellent. Located a short way down the track north from the Ermita de Nuestra Señora de los Reyes (see below).

◆◆
ERMITA DE NUESTRA SEÑORA DE LOS REYES

This is the Hermitage of Our Lady of the Kings, the patroness of the island, whose shrine is a little white church in the plain of La Dehesa in the west.
A row of whitewashed cabins by the church contains simple cells with bed and cooking facilities for pilgrims.
The story is that on 6 January 1546 ship-wrecked sailors offered the image to local shepherds in exchange for food and water. Carrying the image back home, the shepherds looked down to the coast and saw that the ship had miraculously set sail.
The next miracle followed a lengthy drought. The islanders carried the image of the virgin down to Valverde imploring the Deity for rain, and obtained good results, particularly for an island with an average annual rainfall of 12 inches (300mm). Now, every four years (1997, 2001 etc) in commemoration of the miraculous downpour, the image is taken to Valverde in the first weekends in July, with singing, dancing and festivities.

◆
FARO DE ORCHILLA

The Orchilla Lighthouse, at the opposite end of the island from Valverde, at Punta Orchilla, is still a navigational aid for ships coming from Latin America.

The Ermita (hermitage) of La Dehesa houses an image which is said to have worked miracles

The lighthouse itself cannot be visited but there is a tiny beach of black sand near it. If you manage to get down there the reward is a safe swim off a jetty. Another prize is a certificate issued by the tourist office at Valverde testifying that the bearer has been to 'The End of the World'.

FRONTERA
The fertile nucleus of the fruit and wine growing region of El Hierro and administrative centre of the south and west, Frontera is the ideal base for a walking holiday. The free-standing belfry of the village church of Candelaria has been built on a volcanic boulder, and is a local curiosity.

♦
LA RESTINGA
A fishing village on the southern tip of the island, now beginning to attract some tourists. The harbour is protected by an effective but unattractive breakwater, making it possible to swim in calm waters off a small black beach. Clear water off the coast provides good diving, with facilities and tuition available locally. To judge by the amount of new apartment building underway at Restinga, and the bars and restaurants which already exist, this is the nearest thing in El Hierro to a tourist resort. The road north from La Restinga goes through old volcanic craters and lava fields, frequented at weekends by rabbit-hunters with dogs and ferrets. In this weird landscape, strands of lava, known as **Los Lajiales**, have cooled and petrified like coils of rope laid out

The harsh northern coast near the Roques de Salmór

on flat rocks. The cooled lava has also formed caves and tunnels winding down for miles to the sea. These are on private land but every lad in the area knows precisely where the tunnels are and feels free to explore them.

♦♦♦
MIRADOR DE LA PEÑA
Designed by the Lanzarote architect César Manrique in his own distinctive style, this lookout with cliffs falling away on all sides offers outstanding views of the wide sweep of the bay of El Golfo. The *mirador* also houses a restaurant.

A pleasant promenade follows the bay at different levels. Tamaduste is so close to Valverde airport that you can see the control tower, but the light Fokker aircraft on inter-island routes are a point of interest rather than an irritation.

◆
ROQUES DE SALMÓR
These are two huge rocks rising out of the sea north of the Mirador de la Peña viewpoint. For many years they were the focus of attention as the home of huge primeval lizards indigenous to El Hierro and sometimes as long as 40 inches (1m). Publicity made them prey to dealers and collectors and when it became clear they were in danger of extinction they were removed from the Roques de Salmór. A zoo where they can be safely housed and bred while remaining on view to the public is under construction in the small village of Guinea.

Accommodation

Frontera
With only four twin bedrooms, the **Club Puntagrande Hotel**, Las Puntas, 2-star (tel: 55 90 81) is listed in the Guinness Book of Records as the smallest hotel in the world. What it lacks in size, it makes up for in interest and comfort, sitting as it does on a small fist of land stuck out into a wild sea and with an awesome backdrop of mountains. In former days it was a warehouse. The restaurant serves excellent fresh fish. The village of Frontera, 1,150 feet (350m) above the coast has pension and apartments suitable as a base for walking holidays.

◆
POZO DE LA SALUD
2 miles (3km) outside the village of Sabinosa.
Complete with sulphur and radium, the Pozo de la Salud (Well of Health) is the only spring on the island. A spa hotel is currently under construction. Sabinosa itself is a centre of wine production and basket weaving.

◆◆
TAMADUSTE
This is the only village on the island with a seaside resort feel, due largely to its position round a sheltered little bay. Small boats ride at anchor at high tide and children dive off a board protruding from the jetty.

Las Playas Bay
The **Parador de la Isla de El Hierro**, 3-star (tel: 55 80 36) is at the foot of a steep cliff, 7 miles (12km) south from the Puerto de la Estaca. The road ends at the *parador*, so if it is seclusion you are looking for, look no further. The site was chosen from a helicopter by one of Franco's ministers.

Valverde
Boomerang Hotel, 2-star, Doctor Gost, 1 (tel: 55 02 00). Owned by a one-time visitor to Australia, this is the only hotel in Valverde. Comfortable, not luxurious, but with a bar and restaurant.

Tamaduste
Various small apartments, owned by local people, are available for holiday lets.

Restaurants
Frontera area
El Castano, 5 miles (8km) from Frontera and 15 miles (23km) from Valverde on a winding mountain road, specialises in grilled meat. Choose your own and have it cooked over a wood-fired grill. This *asadero* (roastery) is set among chestnut trees and has a rural atmosphere. Popular with locals.

Guarazoca
Local stone and wood, whitewashed walls, masses of plants and running water make it worth stopping to sit in the huge curved windows of the slightly pretentious **Mirador de la Peña Restaurant**. Marvellous views.

La Restinga
El Refugio is a family restaurant specialising in seafood and fresh fish. Mother cooks, father brings in the fish and the grown-up children serve. They also do a takeaway service of delicious avocado mojo sauce. Try also **Casa Juan** and **El Canario**.

Tamaduste
On the edge of the village with black lava fields beyond and mountains beyond those, the **Tamaduste Bar Restaurante** is cheerful and hospitable, the sort of place where the local priest comes in for lunch and watches a bit of television news as well.

Tigaday
Hostal Guanche, near Frontera on the slopes of the El Golfo basin. Here a husband and wife team serve excellent Canarian food in an outwardly unprepossessing bar.

Shopping
The local **cheesecake** (*quesadilla*) enjoys a high reputation. In general, though, this is an island where it is impossible to be a heavy consumer.

Special Events
The **Bajada de la Virgen de los Reyes** (Descent of the Virgin of the Kings) from her shrine in the forests to Valverde. Every fourth year, first weekend in July, 2005, 2009 etc.

Sport
People come to El Hierro for the **walking**. The landscape and the views are wonderful, but a real field day is assured for anyone interested in natural history or geology. For underwater exploration, the **Restinga Dive-In Centre** at La Restinga offers **diving** facilities and tuition. A shop next door sells all the gear.

LA PALMA

General Information

Full name: San Miguel de la Palma. Size: 281 square miles (728sq km). 29 miles (47km) north to south and maximum 18 miles (29km) wide.
Highest point: 7,947 feet (2,423m).
Population: 80,000.

Cool and green, La Palma is the most northwesterly of the Canary Islands. It is small, but in any description of the island, superlatives abound. Its centre is a national park dominated by a huge crater called the Caldera de Taburiente, which is one of the largest in the world. The northern rim of the crater rises to form the island's highest peak at 7,947 feet (2,423m). In relation to the size of the landmass it rises from, it is, according to enthusiasts, the highest peak in the world. East, north and west of the great crater, the land plunges towards the sea in deep ravines. But to the south, Las Cumbres, a ridge of lesser volcanic peaks, makes a raised spine running away down the centre of the land. The Volcán de Teneguía on the island's southernmost tip, still smouldering today, was in 1971 the scene of the most recent eruption in the Canaries. Another striking aspect of La Palma is the overwhelming greenery. The gorges that fall

The compact little capital of Santa Cruz is the island's only sizeable town

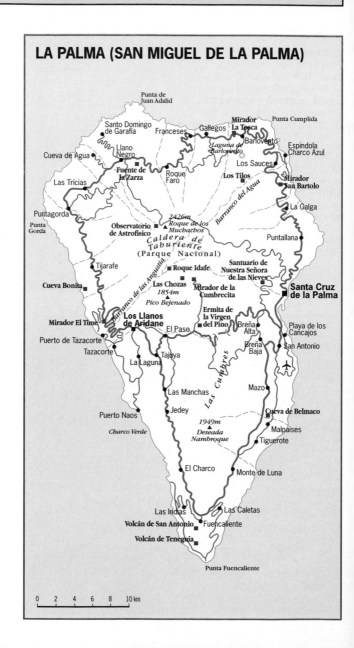

LA PALMA (SAN MIGUEL DE LA PALMA)

Punta de
Juan Adalid

Santo Domingo
de Garafía
Franceses
Gallegos
**Mirador
La Tosca**
Punta Cumplida

*Laguna de
Barlovento*
Barlovento
Espindola
Charco Azul

Cueva de Agua
Llano
Negro
Los Sauces

**Fuente de
la Zarza**
Roque
Faro
Los Tilos
**Mirador
San Bartolo**

Las Tricias
La Galga

Barranco del Agua

Puntagorda
2426m
*Roque de los
Muchachos*
Puntallana

Punta
Gorda
**Observatorio
de Astrofísico**
*Caldera de
Taburiente*
(Parque Nacional)

Tijarafe
Roque Idafe
**Santuario de
Nuestra Señora
de las Nieves**

Cueva Bonita
Las Chozas
1854m
▲
Pico Bejenado
**Mirador de la
Cumbrecita**
**Santa Cruz
de la Palma**

Barranco de las Angustias
**Ermita de
la Virgen
del Pino**

Mirador El Time
**Los Llanos
de Aridane**
El Paso
Breña
Alta
Playa de los
Cancajos

Puerto de Tazacorte
Breña
Baja
San Antonio

Tazacorte
Las Cumbres

La Laguna
Tajuya

Las Manchas
Mazo

Puerto Naos
Jedey

Charco Verde
1949m
▲
*Deseada
Nambroque*
Cueva de Belmaco

Malpaíses

Tiguerote

El Charco
Monte de Luna

Las Indias
Las Caletas

Volcán de San Antonio
Fuencaliente

Volcán de Teneguía

Punta Fuencaliente

0   2   4   6   8   10 km

steeply to the sea are covered with dense woods of pine, myrtle and laurel. Bananas are grown on a grand scale, and avocados and tobacco are on the increase. The coast is rugged, with cliffs dropping abruptly to the sea and a few small beaches of fine black sand. For that reason alone, there are no huge tourist developments on the island.

Island History

La Palma was conquered by Alonso Fernández de Lugo and became a dependency of the Spanish crown in 1493. Granted a licence to trade with America the island soon became a major commercial centre attracting entrepreneurs from the whole of Europe. In the 16th century, the capital, Santa Cruz, was regarded as one of the three most important Spanish ports, exporting cane sugar and building ships. The resultant prosperity made it a ready target for pirates like the English privateer Sir Francis Drake, who was successfully repulsed by cannon fire from the Castillo de Santa Catalina.

RESORTS

PLAYA DE LOS CANCAJOS

3 miles (5km) south of Santa Cruz
This is a recent but growing tourist development on a small, rocky bay of black sand between the airport and the city. The accommodation consists of apartment hotels and apartments, all so far on a modest scale. But the concrete mixers have not finished yet.

PUERTO NAOS

The longest-established tourist development on the west coast of the island, Puerto Naos is surrounded by lava fields and banana plantations and is used mainly by Germans, and Spaniards visiting their holiday apartments from the nearby island of Tenerife. Bars and restaurants are edged by a promenade above a wide beach of black sand, planted with palms. The sea is calm with excellent swimming. **Charco Verde** beach, further south, is traditionally reserved for nude bathing.

SANTA CRUZ DE LA PALMA

Santa Cruz, was founded by Alonso Fernández de Lugo in 1493. It is small and contained within natural limits. Its most interesting old buildings can be found in the couple of streets and squares behind the long stretch of the Avenida Marítima which lines the seaward side of the city. On the Avenida itself there are a number of charming old Canarian houses with decorated wooden balconies, among them the Parador Nacional, which blends into anonymity. A variety of bars and pavement cafés along the Avenida bring the city to life in the evenings.

WHAT TO SEE IN SANTA CRUZ

AYUNTAMIENTO

A former cardinal's palace of the mid-16th century, the Ayuntamiento is now the Town Hall – one of many striking historic buildings on the triangle

*Step inside Santa Cruz town hall
(built 1569) to admire its colourful
murals and outstanding
woodcarving*

made up of the Plaza de España
and the Calle O'Daly. The
exterior is arcaded Italian
Renaissance but the interior is all
dark Canarian wood panelling.
Murals by Mariano de Cossio
depict scenes of local life.

◆
BARCO DE LA
VIRGEN/MUSEO NAVAL
Avenida de las Nieves
A surprising sight at the end of
the Plaza de la Alameda, the
Barco (Ship) is a life-size
concrete replica of Columbus's
Santa María, its prow facing the
sea. The maritime museum
situated in the hold of the ship is
not very interesting, but it is
worth going through the two
floors of exhibits to emerge on

the deck of the *Santa María* with
its sudden view of the sea.
Open: Monday to Friday
9.30–13.00, 16.00–19.30hrs.
Closed: weekends.

◆◆
IGLESIA DEL SALVADOR
Plaza de España
A 16th-century church at the top
of a noble stone staircase. There
is a fine Moorish-style
(*artesonado*) ceiling in the nave
and an unusual example of
Gothic vaulting in the sacristy.
The impressive but non-
functioning fountain beside the
church was built on the site of
the first Cabildo or Regional
Council of the island, which in
turn was formerly the meeting
place of the elders of the pre-
Hispanic people of the island.
Open: daily, 08.30–13.00,
16.00–20.30hrs.

◆◆
IGLESIA DE SAN FRANCISCO/
MUSEO INSULAR
Calle de San Francisco
The 16th-century church is also
the site of the Island Museum
covering natural history,
ethnography and fine art.
Exhibits include remains of
Guanche artefacts, ecclesiastical
vestments and treasures.
Open: Monday to Friday
09.30–13.00hrs, 16.00–19.30hrs.

WHAT TO SEE OUTSIDE
SANTA CRUZ

###
BARLOVENTO
Barlovento is a substantial
agricultural town on the
northeast tip of the island. The
parish church was built in the

17th century. Three-quarters of a mile (1km) west from Barlovento there are signposts to the **Laguna de Barlovento**, officially described as the largest artificial lake on the island. It was designed as a water reservoir and will fulfil its secondary function as a beauty spot when the problem of water seepage is solved. At the moment it is a dry lake.

The road to the west tunnels through gorges and climbs and descends through wooded hills of great loveliness. Steep tracks wind their way down to isolated little fishing villages like **Gallegos** and **Franceses** which are hardly visited and untouched by tourism.

◆◆
BARRANCO DE LAS ANGUSTIAS

This long gorge on the west side of the Caldera de Taburiente drains water from the crater in a series of streams and waterfalls. The name means 'gorge of anguish': it was the scene of the resistance of Tanasu, the only Guanche leader on the island who did not capitulate to the Spanish invaders. After a siege of seven months he was tricked into captivity and, refusing to eat or drink, died on his way to Spain. Serious walkers often enter the Caldera de Taburiente park from here and it is also possible to hike to the **Roque Idafe**, a monolithic basalt column, an important religious symbol to the Guanches.

CALDERA DE TABURIENTE
see **PARQUE NACIONAL DE LA CALDERA DE TABURIENTE**

◆
CUEVA BONITA

A seawater grotto on the west coast of the island, it is reached by fishing boat from Tazacorte. The trip takes about three hours and operates on a fairly casual basis, depending on the weather and number of takers.

◆
EL PASO

The silk and cigar centre of La Palma, El Paso is a prosperous town east of Los Llanos in the centre of the island. The tobacco industry is doing well but silk manufacture has declined since the 18th century when there were over 3,000 looms on the island. If there are no signs to the silk-making, ask for directions to the house of Señora Bertila Pérez Gonzales. See **Shopping**, below.

◆◆◆
FUENCALIENTE

20 miles (33km) south of Santa Cruz
Named after the hot thermal spring (*fuente caliente*) which disappeared under the volcanic lava of the eruption of San Antonio in 1667, this town stands on the southernmost tip of the island. It is famous for vines cultivated in the volcanic ash on the hillsides around, producing the much admired Malvasía wine, or Malmsey. A short walk down from the town takes you to the 2,156-foot- (657m) high San Antonio volcano, from where you can also see below the smouldering Volcán de Teneguía, site of the archipelago's most recent eruption in 1971. It is possible to walk right round Volcán de San Antonio and to the rim of Volcán de Teneguiá.

THE WESTERN ISLANDS – LA PALMA

The San Antonio volcano formed this crater in an eruption in 1667. It lies a short walk away from Fuencaliente

◆
FUENTE DE LA ZARZA

This is the site of ancient rock inscriptions of circles and loops, whose origins and significance remain a mystery. It is reached by a 10-minute walk along a footpath west of the village of Roque Faro in the north of the island. Ask at the village for directions. This area is the centre of goat-rearing, and beyond Roque Faro the only

other human you are likely to see on this road is a goatherd with his flock, or someone gathering piles of pine-needles for animal bedding and compost.

◆◆◆
LA CUMBRECITA

A viewpoint located as far into the heart of the Caldera as it is possible to go by road. From Santa Cruz heading west, the road leads through the Tunel de la Cumbre and winds up through pine forests. The view from the *mirador* at La Cumbrecita is spectacular

old centre of town. Instead, turn right here (heading from Santa Cruz) and you will find a charming plaza with an early 16th-century church, Iglesia de los Remedios, a typically Canarian *ayuntamiento* (town hall) and café tables and chairs spreading beneath ancient Indian laurel trees.

Step behind the church and there are more fine old houses and a view of the mountains.

LOS TILOS

An area of ancient woodland, mostly of lime, laurel, myrtle trees and giant ferns, it lies along the Barranco del Agua just south of Los Sauces. This area is of such environmental and botanical interest that it is under UNESCO protection.

MAZO

A little south and west of the airport lies Mazo, the pottery centre of the island. A workshop housed in an old mill, **El Molino**, displays and sells rough earthenware pots made without a wheel and decorated with the designs found on early Guanche pottery. In the same village the church, Iglesia de San Blás, is notable for its fine altar and carvings dating from the 16th century.

when it is clear. But if all you can see is clouds, try the *mirador* a little further west at **Las Chozas**: there can be quite different weather conditions within a short distance on La Palma. From La Cumbrecita or Las Chozas the bottom of the crater is about four or five hours' walk away, but is not a trip to make without a guide.

LOS LLANOS DE ARIDANE

It is easy to drive along the dual carriageway that bypasses Los Llanos and completely miss the

MIRADOR SAN BARTOLO

The view from this lookout on a small headland north of Santa Cruz is of many deep-cut ravines covered in woods or terraced for agriculture, dotted with small white houses and

Banana plantations lead down to the sea from the characterful old town of Tazacorte

falling down sharply to the rugged coast. The villages here are small and peaceful, almost deserted; the dog lying in the middle of the road will slowly shamble to the side to let you pass and only bark a warning at you when you are safely gone. Northwards through thick green banana plantations hissing with irrigation pipes is **Charco Azul** ('the blue pool'), a pleasantly situated semi-natural lido protected by rocks for relatively calm bathing – the rest of the coast is very wild. There's a cheerful bar and restaurant here too. The track through the same dense banana terraces continues past sheds where men trim and pack the fruit and on to the fishing village of **Espindola** with boats drawn up on a black shingly

beach surrounded by high cliffs. A large number of concrete blocks lying around the harbour make this a less picturesque place than it might be.

OBSERVATORIO DE ASTROFISICO

The clear atmosphere and cloudless nights at Roque de los Muchachos (the highest point on the rim of the Caldera de Taburiente), was the reason for siting the Astrophysical Observatory here. The observatory, one of the most important in the world, is maintained by several European countries to provide research facilities in the field of astrophysics. It is not generally open to the public (tel: 40 55 00 for summer tour details) but you can catch a glimpse of its space-age buildings on the way to the Roque de los Muchachos.

♦♦♦
PARQUE NACIONAL DE LA CALDERA DE TABURIENTE ✓

This national park is a huge crater – La Caldera – which was formed some 400,000 years ago in a massive explosion. It is over 5 miles (9km) across at its widest point and has a circumference of 17 miles (28km). Its highest point, at Roque de los Muchachos, is 7,977 feet (2,426m). The crater dominates the island, and its stark, bare peaks stand out from pine-covered slopes rising from laurel and myrtle woods. This is an area of great interest for botanists, geologists and zoologists, vulcanologists and holiday-makers.
Whether walking or driving (there is only one surfaced road leading into the park) the park is small but extraordinary. At the southeastern approach to the crater, there is a sign to the **Ermita de la Virgen del Pino**, the hermitage church of the Virgin of the Pines. The setting of this little white building in the pine-covered hillside is worth the small detour.

♦
PUNTAGORDA
17 miles (28km) north of Los Llanos de Aridane
This sparsely inhabited, straggling agricultural settlement lacks any real centre. The village produces almonds, flowers, fruit and vegetables and the surrounding fields are particularly pretty in the spring, when the pink almond trees are in blossom.

♦
SAN ANDRÉS Y LOS SAUCES
17 miles (28km) north of Santa Cruz
The top half of this twinned village, Los Sauces, is a modern agricultural centre of little interest. Take the road down through the dense banana plantations to San Andrés, where you will find a charming square shared by a 17th-century church, well-tended gardens and a popular fish restaurant. From here old houses tumble down the steep cobbled hill towards the sea.

♦♦
SANTUARIO DE NUESTRA SEÑORA DE LAS NIEVES
In the hills 2 miles (3.5km) west of Santa Cruz stands the most important religious building on the island: the Shrine of Our Lady of the Snows. This small, white, 17th-century church with Canarian balconies, in a square surrounded by flamboyant trees, houses the figure of the patron saint of the island. The terracotta image, dressed in grand robes on an ornate silver altar, dates from the 14th century and is one of the oldest religious objects in the Canaries. Every five years – the next date is in the year 2005 – there takes place *La Bajada de la Virgen* (The Descent of the Virgin), when the image is taken down to Santa Cruz.

♦♦
TAZACORTE
It was here, on 29 September 1492, that the Castillian forces under Alonso Fernández de Lugo first landed on the island.

Now the town is a peaceful and industrious centre of banana production and fishing. There has been some dismal modern building but Tazacorte retains grand old 16th-century houses. The streets immediately behind the main thoroughfare are small, cobbled passages threading through the slopes of the town.

There is a small beach used by locals down a side road at the north end of town by the church. Continuing north, the fishing harbour is a busy focal point, and with plans to build a swimming pool near by it looks as though it will continue to develop. Good fish restaurants are also springing up.

Accommodation
Playa de los Cancajos
Apartmentos Costa Salinas (tel: 43 43 48) is a new, smart complex of apartments attached to the 4-star **Hotel Taburiente Playa** (tel: 18 12 77). Facilities include a swimming pool, supermarket and disco. The **Hacienda San Jorge** apartments (tel: 18 10 66) are built to the traditional design of a local artist, and are set in gardens with seawater swimming pool, gym and sauna facilities.
Centro Cancajos (tel: 18 13 00) are pleasant apartments built around a swimming pool. The **Lago Azul** (tel: 43 51 28) is very similar.

Puerto Naos
The 4-star **Sol La Palma** (tel: 40 80 00), is far and away the island's most luxurious and biggest (300 rooms) hotel.

Santa Cruz
Hotel San Miguel, Avenida José Antonio 31, 3-star (tel: 41 12 43). Large hotel in centre of town. Often used by walkers. Cheerful and friendly. **Parador de Santa Cruz de la Palma,** Avenida Marítima 34, (tel: 41 23 40). A large colonial-style house, not as luxurious as some *paradores*, but reliable and comfortable.

Nightlife and Entertainment
Very limited. 'Nightclub' is often the local euphemism for a place of ill repute. **Disco Aquarium** at Los Llanos de Aridane is widely regarded as the best on the island. Here also is one other disco and several bars.
Melody is a popular karaoke bar in Puerto de Naos.

Restaurants
Los Cancajos
La Fontana and **Havana** are both recommended for good cooking and a pleasant atmosphere. **El Pulpo**, on the beach, may look a shack but it serves excellent seafood.

Los Llanos de Aridane
San Petronio is an Italian restaurant just outside the town, run by an Italian and Flemish couple who speak all the major European languages between them. Popular with locals.

Santa Cruz
Restaurante Canarias on the Avenida Marítima offers real Canarian food. There are many other bars and restaurants along the Avenida which come to life in the evening and where you can sit, drink and eat *tapas* – the tasty little Spanish snacks.

A vortex cloud above the Caldera de Taburiente. It dominates the view from Tazacorte, a peaceful centre for banana growing

Tazacorte
Playa Mont is an excellent fresh fish restaurant situated down by the harbour. Eat inside or out among the palms and papaya trees in the courtyard.
Try also **Monte Cristo** – the exterior may look rather shabby but the food served here is top class.

Shopping
A frequent boast here is that the local cigars are better than Havana's, their Cuban counterpart. You can test that assertion at any tobacconist.
La Palma is claimed to be the only place in Spain where **silk** is still produced by traditional methods. The centre of this small cottage industry is in **El Paso**, but the workshop here, Casa de Sericultura (tel: 48 56 92), is more often closed than open. Unfortunately the traditional skills of silk-making are dying out on the island.
Pots shaped by hand without a wheel and based on traditional Guanche designs are sold at **El Molino** mill in Mazo, on the east coast. This is a very small, government-encouraged enterprise (tel: 44 02 13).

Special Events
The Festival of Nuestra Señora de las Nieves (Our Lady of the Snows) is celebrated on 5 August each year. Every five years (the next is in the year 2005) the whole of August is given over to celebrating *La Bajada de la Virgen*, the Descent of the Virgin, from her shrine in Las Nieves to the Ship of the Virgin in Santa Cruz. There is singing, dancing, plays performed, cannons fired, processions in the street and the whole of La Palma celebrates.

THE EASTERN ISLANDS: GRAN CANARIA, FUERTEVENTURA AND LANZAROTE

GRAN CANARIA

General Information
Size: 592 square miles (1,532sq km). Almost circular, diameter approx 27½ miles (44km), circuit of island approx 126 miles (200km).
Highest point: Pico de las Nieves, 6,395 feet (1,949m).
Population: 700,000.

Gran Canaria was once the most popular tourist destination of the Canary Islands and is often called Las Palmas after its main city – the biggest in the archipelago with a population of 400,000. It used to be the Canary Islands' most fashionable resort too, and still is very lively, but these days the majority of visitors head straight for the south, to the pulse and throb of the nightclubs in the beach resorts of Playa del Inglés and Maspalomas. Apart from these spots of high activity, the rest of the island is entirely Canarian.
After Tenerife and Fuerteventura, it is the third largest island in the group – but it is possible to drive around the whole island in a single day. The lasting impression is one of contrasts. Gran Canaria is often called 'a continent in miniature'; a reference to the extremes of landscape and climate that may be found on this island. Its landscapes change quickly from Wild West canyons to idyllic pine forests to Sahara-like dunes, and while there may be a dusting of snow on Pico de las Nieves, Maspalomas will still be wallowing in sun.
In shape, the island is an almost perfect circle with the highest volcanic peaks in the middle. Forests of laurel, chestnut and pine descend to green slopes of banana plantations and farming valleys. To the west, the land falls sharply from the centre to the sea in deep *barrancos* or gorges; to the north it remains high and green and ends suddenly in steep, rugged cliffs. In the most populated part, to the south and east, the high places level down into an arid plain fringed by wide sandy beaches.
The main source of income for the island since the 1960s has been tourism. The benefits are there for all to see. The disadvantages are equally obvious. Complaints that ugly, ill-conceived and badly designed resorts have destroyed parts of the landscape are heard more often on Gran Canaria than on any other island.

Island History
Jean de Béthencourt took Lanzarote, Fuerteventura and El Hierro for the Spanish throne in 1405. When he attempted to subdue Gran Canaria, he failed. It was not until 1478 that a further attempt was made by Juan Rejón. He landed on the island and founded the town of Ciudad Real de Las Palmas (Royal City of the Palms) from which he set out to subdue the remainder of the island.
Gran Canaria at the time was

ruled by Guanche kings, or *guanartemes*, who proved redoubtable leaders of the resistance. Even when they realised the futility of their struggle, many Guanches preferred to throw themselves from high cliffs and die rather than be taken. It was not until 1483 that the Spaniards could claim they had succeeded in imposing their authority on the whole island. The next important date is 1492 when Columbus used Gran Canaria as a staging post on his first voyage to the New World. The advantages of its position in relation to the Americas, Africa and Europe, plus the growth of trade in sugar and wine

exports, brought the island growing prosperity throughout the 16th and 17th centuries. However, this in its turn brought the penalty of constant attack from pirates. Las Palmas, on the coast, was a prime target. Fortresses and defensive walls to the north and south of the city proved barely adequate to the task of defence. In 1927 the Canary Islands were divided into two provinces, with Las Palmas de Gran Canaria as head of the eastern province, including Lanzarote and Fuerteventura.

The sandy beach makes Puerto Rico ideal for watersports or just lounging in the sun

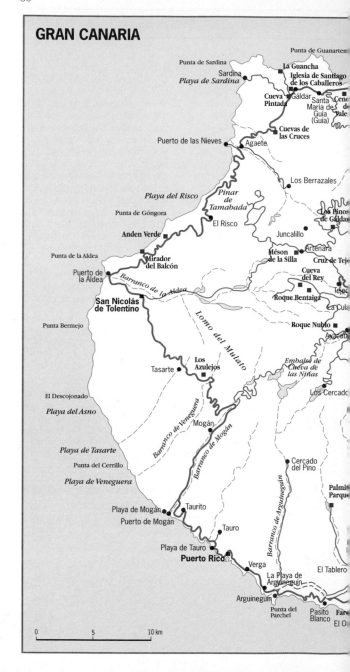

GRAN CANARIA

Punta de Guanarteme

Punta de Sardina
Sardina
Playa de Sardína

La Guancha
Iglesia de Santiago
de los Caballeros

Cueva
Pintada
Gáldar
Cene
d
Vale

Santa
Maria de
Guía
(Guía)

Cuevas de
las Cruces

Puerto de las Nieves
Agaete

Los Berrazales

Playa del Risco
Pinar de Tamabada

Los Pinos
de Gáldar

Punta de Góngora

Anden Verde
El Risco

Juncalillo

Artenara

Punta de la Aldea

Mirador
del Balcón

Méson
de la Silla

Cruz de Tej

Cueva
del Rey

Puerto de
la Aldea
Barranco de la Aldea

Tejec

San Nicolás
de Tolentino

Roque Bentaiga

La Cula

Lomo del Mulato

Punta Bermejo

Roque Nublo

Ayaca

Los
Azulejos

Tasarte

*Embalse de
Cueva de
las Niñas*

Los Cercad

El Descojonado
Playa del Asno

Barranco de Veneguera

Barranco de Mogán

Mogán

Playa de Tasarte
Punta del Cerrillo
Playa de Veneguera

Cercado
del Pino

Barranco de Arguineguín

Palmi
Parqu

Playa de Mogán
Taurito
Puerto de Mogán

Tauro

Playa de Tauro
Puerto Rico

Verga

El Tablero

La Playa de
Arguineguín

Arguineguín

Punta del
Parchel

Pasito
Blanco

Far
El O

0   5   10 km

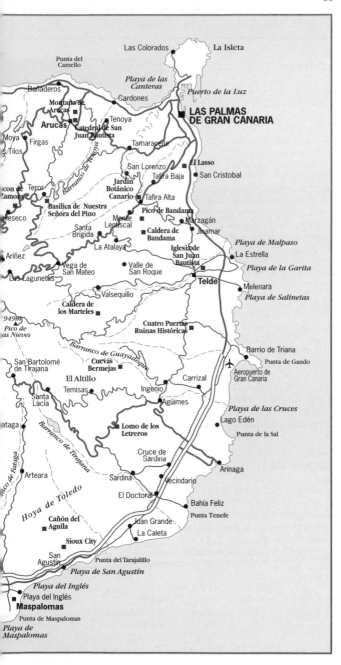

RESORTS

ARGUINEGUÍN/PATALÁVACA
6 miles (10km) west of Maspalomas
Arguineguín, not to be confused with the adjacent high-density resort of La Playa de Arguineguín/Patalávaca, is the original fishing village from which this resort grew. There is a daily fish auction at the port and Tuesday is market day. The white sandy beach of **Patalávaca**, a little further west, is delightful and seems to be used as a spillover from the main resort.

◆ BAHÍA FELIZ
This is the newest resort (or 'urbanisation') as you hit the south of Gran Canaria on the east coast motorway. The facilities are all there – hotels, apartments, shops and restaurants – but the beach is decidedly black and small. Most people swim in their hotel pools and sunbathe on hotel terraces. Good for windsurfing.

◆◆◆ LAS PALMAS
This city was a holiday destination patronised by the British long before any other development on the island. Now, as well as serving its commercial and maritime functions, it is a busy, rather faded cosmopolitan resort, with a dense area of hotels – ranging from 5-star to red-light – shops, bars and restaurants lining the 1½-mile (2.4km) beach of Las Canteras. Offshore reefs which form a natural volcanic barrier make this beach safe for swimming as

The Casa de Colón in Las Palmas was used as a stopover by Columbus en route to the New World

well as for practising the various water-sports that are available. Because Las Canteras is a town beach patronised during summer weekends by locals, it can become extremely crowded. The population is also periodically swelled by sailors. Away from the beach area, the historic sights of the town are mostly concentrated in a small area of the old town, La Vegueta, in the south of the city. (See also Las Palmas, **What to See**, below.)

◆◆◆ MASPALOMAS
Maspalomas is by far the largest tourist development in the Canaries. It is an amalgam of

three formerly separate resorts. Running east to west, as first experienced by visitors arriving from the airport, these are **San Agustín**, **Playa del Inglés** and **Maspalomas** proper. They lie about an hour's drive from Las Palmas on the four lane motorway down the eastern coast. Extraordinarily rapid development has taken place here since the 1960s, taking advantage of the sunny weather of the south – claimed locally as 350 days of sunshine – and over 4 miles (6km) of sandy beaches. At the southern extreme, these end in a peninsula of Saharan-style sand dunes, brilliant white and one of the most beautiful features of the whole of the Canaries. From the motorway, however, first impressions are of concrete and advertisements,

apartments and hotels, with regular and increasingly insistent signs to individual tourist *urbanizaciones*.

San Agustín

The earliest development on this stretch of coast, San Agustín still considers itself a cut above the rest. Together with a range of important hotels and low-rise apartments with pretty gardens, good restaurants and a quiet beach of dark volcanic sand, it deliberately cultivates a classy and restrained demeanour, at least in comparison with the more robust Playa del Inglés.

Playa del Inglés

The density of apartment and hotel building is daunting until you find your way around this super-compressed tourist city. It is lively and energetic, with everything a mass-market holiday consumer might expect. Transport is efficient and easy: buses run through the resort linking beach, hotels and shopping areas. There is also an electric 'roadtrain' called the Maspalomas Express which operates through the main streets.

Playa de Maspalomas

Separated from the Playa del Inglés by sand dunes which have been designated an official area of natural interest, this is a much smaller resort and, for some, the most elegant of them all. Certainly there are some very fine hotels here and the atmosphere is not so unashamedly boisterous as elsewhere. Tall palms and well-cultivated gardens provide a lush and restful scene. But then,

The sand dunes of Maspalomas are protected from development

before the days of tourism, this was actually an oasis.

◆ PASITO BLANCO

on the western side of the Maspalomas lighthouse (Faro de Maspalomas)
This is an up-market private development of apartments around a marina in an attractive cove. Visitors can leave their cars and walk down to the jetty to watch the big game fishing boats unload their catch on summer afternoons.

◆◆◆ PUERTO DE MOGÁN

20 miles (32km) west of Maspalomas
Puerto de Mogán is a model example of sympathetic Canarian holiday development. The old fishing harbour has been expanded to a traffic-free 'village' of local-style houses, painted white with a pastel trim, each with a wrought-iron balcony and pretty window boxes or garden. The houses cluster around a new pleasure marina, joined coherently by arches and bridges, and shops, bars and restaurants are well-kept. The original fishing fleet is still here and gives a genuine local touch to the marina. There is a small black beach next to the port but most visitors prefer to make the short boat trip to the golden sands of Puerto Rico (see below).

◆◆ PUERTO RICO

some 10 miles (15km) west of Maspalomas beach
Puerto Rico has become a byword for watersports. With a man-made beach, two lidos and a 600-berth marina in a well

protected bay, this is an excellent resort for those who enjoy sailing, deep sea fishing, windsurfing, scuba diving and the like. Olympic gold medalists train at the sailing school here. There are many non-sporting visitors as well, and massive new building programmes have obliterated both sides of the hill surrounding the original resort. On the road continuing west from Puerto Rico to Puerto de Mogán, there is new tourist development round every headland, clinging to clifftops, or rising from dry river beds.

LAS PALMAS ✓

This lively, bustling city has many roles. It is a commercial centre, one of Spain's major ports, and a considerable resort. This is where Columbus stayed on his first voyage of discovery, where the oldest historic buildings of the Canaries are to be found and where the serious cultural life of the island is lived. It has two centres, the beach and harbour at one end and the old town at the other. Each has expanded so that the two have met in the middle. The overspill is contained on land reclaimed from the sea and in a new town added on the hills behind. Walking or driving (if you can negotiate the appalling traffic) between these two major points of reference leads through most areas of interest.

The best place to start is the port. This is always a hub of activity with all sorts of vessel from many different countries. Across the narrowest point of the Isleta peninsula, the great beach of Las Canteras stretches 1½ miles (2.4km) to the west along a boulevard busy with bars, restaurants, shops and hotels. This is the major resort area of Las Palmas.

Almost directly opposite the Santa Catalina quay in the port is the Santa Catalina park, busy enough during the day with its open air cafés and shops but coming into its own in the evening. Late at night though, this area can appear decidedly sinister. Moving further west there is the Canarian parliament building, and south of that lies the major shopping area on Avenida de Mesa y Lopez, where you will find specialist shops as well as department stores like El Corte Inglés. The beach immediately facing this area, Las Alcaravaneras, is too close to all the activities of a busy port to be recommended for swimming. Further south through the gardens and parks of the affluent residential area of the Ciudad Jardín, you come to the Parque Doramas, a green oasis with huge palm trees and fountains. The 5-star Santa Catalina Hotel, the Néstor Museum and the Pueblo Canario (Canarian Village) stand in the park. From here you can walk through busy city streets to the Parque de San Telmo with its ancient dragon trees. This forms the boundary of the pedestrianised shopping area of Triana. Every style of architecture from Spanish colonial to Modernism is to be found among the buildings here. Five minutes walk down the Mayor de Triana across the Guiniguada ravine brings you to

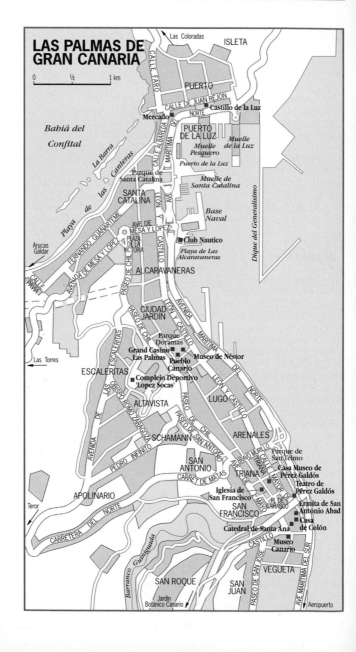

the **Vegueta** district of the old town. Within this small area are concentrated all the most interesting historical monuments of the city.

WHAT TO SEE IN LAS PALMAS

◆◆◆
CASA DE COLÓN
Calle de Colón 1, Vegueta
The 'Columbus House' is a beautiful old 15th-century building, formerly the residence of the island's first governor, Pedro de Vera. Columbus stayed here in 1492 preparing for his first voyage to America, and again the following year. The house is now a museum dedicated to his travels and discoveries in the New World. It also contains paintings from the Prado in Madrid.
Open: Monday to Friday 09.00–19.00hrs; Saturday and Sunday 09.00–15.00hrs.
Closed: Public holidays.

◆
CASA MUSEO DE PÉREZ GALDÓS
Calle Cano 6, Triana
Benito Pérez Galdós, a prolific Spanish writer and novelist, was born in this house in 1843 and lived and died here. He was a tireless advocate of social reform. The public rooms downstairs have been turned into a library and a lecture hall. Exhibits include various personal effects of the author including his death mask.
Open: Monday to Friday 09.00–20.00hrs;
Saturday 10.00–18.00hrs;
Sunday 10.00–15.00hrs.

The writer's name is also given to the nearby Opera House, the **Teatro Pérez Galdós**, Lentini 1. This is the undisputed musical focus of the island. Every performance of any significance in Las Palmas takes place at this venue.

◆
CASTILLO DE LA LUZ
Calle Juan Réjon, Isleta
The defensive fortress beside the fishing harbour of Puerto de la Luz is the oldest historical monument on the island. It was built by Alonso Fajardo in 1494. French, Dutch and English pirates, including Sir Francis Drake, were successfully repulsed. Now, the fortress is a cultural centre, a venue for exhibitions, lectures, concerts and recitals.

◆
CATEDRAL DE SANTA ANA
Plaza Santa Ana, Vegueta
Facing the town hall in the Plaza de Santa Ana, the cathedral was begun at the end of the 15th century but not finished until the beginning of the 20th.
The treasures of the cathedral include works by Canary artists and craftsmen, including the 18th-century goldsmith José Eugenio and the sculptor José Luján Pérez. Many other examples of religious art and sculpture, and curiously enough, French porcelain, are housed in the Museo Diocesano de Arte Sacro (small entrance charge).
Museum open: Monday to Friday 10.00–16.30hrs;
Saturday 10.00–13.30hrs.
Closed: Sunday and festivals.

The Parque Doramas, a welcome respite from the traffic and hustle and bustle of Las Palmas

ERMITA DE SAN ANTONIO ABAD

Vegueta

An 18th-century baroque church, built on the site of the first church in Las Palmas, where Christopher Columbus attended mass before he set off on his first voyage to the New World. The old streets and squares of Santo Domingo and Espiritu Santo around here are particularly attractive.

◆◆

MUSEO CANARIO

Calle Dr Chil 25, Vegueta

The most important collection of Guanche artefacts is housed at this Museum of the Canaries. It includes domestic and agricultural tools, pottery, *pintaderas* (early terracotta seals) and carved figures. There are also 16th-century maps of Canarian towns by Leonardo Torriani and models of Guanche people and their villages. An impressive display of skulls runs the length of one large room, with piles of arthritic bones. The Guanches were talented embalmers: mummies wrapped in layers of skin are displayed in glass cases, still showing hunks of hair, nails and even entrails. *Open*: Monday to Friday 10.00–20.00hrs; Saturday and Sunday 10.00–14.00hrs. *Closed*: Public holidays.

MUSEO DE NÉSTOR
Parque Doramas
Within the Pueblo Canario (Canarian Village) on one side of the square stands the house of the modernist painter who designed it, Néstor de la Torre. Pleasant and light, the whole house is a permanent exhibition of his sketches, paintings and theatrical set designs.
Open: Tuesday to Saturday 10.00–20.00hrs; Sunday 10.30–14.30hrs.
Closed: Monday and holidays.

◆◆
PUEBLO CANARIO
Parque Doramas
A re-creation of a typical Canarian village in the grounds of Parque Doramas by the modernist Canarian painter, Néstor de la Torre. It is all fake, but a pleasant enough place to drink sangría, buy souvenirs and samples of local crafts, and attend displays of folk dancing and singing.
Performances take place on Thursday evenings, 17.30–19.00hrs, and Saturday mornings 11.30–13.00hrs. Also on Sunday mornings, keen philatelists run a busy market and exchange of stamps in the Pueblo.

WHAT TO SEE OUTSIDE LAS PALMAS

◆◆
AGAETE
26 miles (41km) west of Las Palmas
This town at the mouth of the Barranco de Agaete is the centre of the most fertile area of the island, growing papaya, coffee, mango and avocados. About

half a mile (1km) west, the little port of **Puerto de las Nieves**, once important for shipping the agricultural produce of the area, is now better known for its fish restaurants and the extraordinary rock formation on its coast, the **Dedo de Dios** (Finger of God).

Rain-making Ceremony
The Concepción church contains M16th-century Flemish triptych which is on display only during the annual festivities of the *Bajada de la Rama* – the Descent of the Branch, 4–7 August. A survival of the ancient Guanche ceremony for invoking rain, the Descent involves a daybreak climb to the great pine forests of Tamadaba, high above this northern coast. Villagers bring down branches and use them to beat the sea for rain.

◆◆
ARUCAS
11 miles (18km) west of Las Palmas
Arucas is the third largest town on the island, set in lush hills of banana and sugar cane plantations. The rum factory produces over 50,000 bottles a day. The town itself is dominated by the huge black church of San Juan Bautista, a neo-Gothic building begun in 1909 and finished in the 1970s. The municipal gardens near the church have an interesting variety of tropical plants. The original Guanche settlement was called Arehucas and the hill to the north of the town is the scene of the final defeat of the Guanche king Doramas, tricked and slain in single combat.

◆◆◆
CALDERA DE BANDAMA ✓

*6 miles (10km) south of
Las Palmas*
The road climbs through
prosperous rolling hills and the
wine growing district of El Monte,
up to the Caldera de Bandama –
the Bandama Crater. The views
from the height of Bandama peak
1,870 feet (569m) are beautiful,
taking in the east coast of the
island, the town of Las Palmas
and, right below, the crater: over
half a mile (1km) wide and
650 feet (200m) deep. Apart from
its dimensions, there is nothing to
remind you that this is a crater
caused by a huge volcanic
explosion. All is rural peace and
quiet. The farm on the floor of the
crater is reached by a track
down the side. This green, fertile
area was much favoured by early
British visitors who constructed
the 18-hole **Bandama golf
course** at the turn of the century –
the first in Spain. Neighbouring
towns like **Santa Brígida** and
Tafira are popular with the well-
to-do of Las Palmas.

*The view from Cruz de Tejeda
includes snowy Teide on Tenerife*

◆◆
CENOBIO DE VALERÓN

18 miles (26km) west of Las Palmas
East of Guía on the old coast
road, this network of about 500
caves is set into steep hillsides
overlooking a ravine. Signs are
inadequate and it is easy to drive
past. The purpose of the caves is
not known for sure, but the most
likely explanation is that they
were used for storing grain.
The circle of stones on the flat
hillside above the Cenobio,
called the **Tagoror**, is where the
ancient governing councils of the
Guanches met. The view of the
coast from here is superb.
Open: Wednesday to Sunday
10.00–17.00hrs.
Closed: Monday and Tuesday.

◆◆◆
CRUZ DE TEJEDA ✓

*27 miles (43km) southwest of
Las Palmas*
A popular place from which to
view the highest peaks on the
island and beyond. Reached by
a route climbing through
eucalyptus, pine and chestnut-

covered hills, this is the only place outside the southern beaches where you will encounter more fellow visitors than you might care for.

The **Cruz de Tejeda** *parador* (no accommodation available) serves a leisurely lunch away from the souvenir and snack stalls, but avoid eating on the terrace. From its rear terrace you can see the two remarkable volcanic rocks, Roque Nublo and Roque Bentayga, which were of religious significance to the Guanches. In the distance is the snowy tip of Mount Teide on the island of Tenerife.

◆
GÁLDAR
19 miles (31km) west of Las Palmas

The town has a charming square, the Plaza de Santiago, a town hall and the church of Santiago de los Caballeros. The town hall is famous for the antiquity of the dragon tree in its courtyard, and the church for the font which witnessed the forced baptism of many Guanches. Otherwise it is a fairly unremarkable place but there are several important Guanche sites outside the town.

La Guancha, a mile (1.5km) from Gáldar is a Guanche burial place. Take a right turn along the

Sardina road from the town and following the signs. To judge by the mummies found within it, the circular area of stones was where important, perhaps royal, Guanches were buried.

◆
GUÍA
18 miles (28km) west of Las Palmas
On the northwest of the island, this small town maintains its identity as a centre for locally produced cheese called *queso de flor* (goat's cheese flavoured with flowers), pottery and decorated knife handles. Most importantly it was the birthplace of the great Canarian sculptor Luján Pérez, whose figure of Nuestra Señora de las Mercedes (Our Lady of Mercies) is in the parish church of Santa María.

Perfectly-carved wooden balconies can be seen in the pretty town of Teror

◆◆
JARDÍN BOTÁNICO CANARIO
La Calzada, near Tafira Alta, 4½ miles (7km) southwest of Las Palmas
The Botanic Garden was the brainchild of Swedish botanist, Erik Sventenius. He was concerned with showing the variety of plant life in the Canaries as well as rescuing those species in danger of extinction. Opened in 1952, plants such as Canarian palms and trees of the laurasilver forest have been grown in as natural a habitat as possible.
Open: Monday to Sunday 09.00–18.00

◆◆◆
PALMITOS PARQUE
5 miles (9km) north of Maspalomas
The sound of running streams and the shade of the huge palms are a sufficient incentive

to visit this otherwise bare corner of the island. The subtropical oasis and park in the Palmitos ravine is home to a fascinating wild bird and butterfly sanctuary. African crested cranes, flamingoes and honey-eaters in well-designed aviaries share the park with domestic fowl and peacocks, and free-flying parrots chatter overhead in the palm trees. In the butterfly house, a carefully controlled environment supports a variety of butterflies, while brilliantly coloured macaws perform tricks for audiences in shows running throughout the day.
Open: daily, 09.30–18.00hrs.

◆
TELDE
9 miles (14km) south of Las Palmas
This is Gran Canaria's second city and was formerly the stronghold of Doramas, the ancient Guanche chief. There is nothing of interest in the modern town, but the 16th-century town of narrow cobbled streets and old Canarian houses is well worth visiting, a memorial to the days when Telde was building its fortunes out of the sugar-cane trade. Among the historic buildings is the 15th-century church of San Juan Bautista (John the Baptist) containing a beautiful carved Flemish altarpiece.

◆◆◆
TEROR
13 miles (21km) down route C-817 from Las Palmas
Set in the centre of the island, the well-preserved, graceful old Canarian town of Teror is all whitewashed houses and carved wooden balconies. It is well named 'The town of balconies'. The Basilica de Nuestra Señora del Pino (Our Lady of the Pines), patroness of the island, stands in the centre of the town. This church was built in the 18th century to commemorate the appearance in 1481 of an effigy of the Virgin in the branches of a pine tree. For a small charge you can visit the treasury.
The **Casa de los Patrónos de la Virgen del Pino** stands in the square of the basilica. Once an 18th-century house, it is now a museum of Canarian furniture and domestic items.
Open: Monday to Thursday and Saturday 11.00–18.00hrs; Sunday 10.00–14.00hrs.
Closed: Friday
Teror is well worth visiting for the landscape in which it stands. The winding mountain road, lined with eucalyptus trees, curls round small villages overlooking steep ravines.

Accommodation
Las Palmas
The city provides a great variety. Luxurious 5-star hotels include:
Meliá Las Palmas on the Calle Gomera (tel: 26 76 00); **Reina Isabel**, Calle Alfredo L Jones (tel: 26 01 00). For a more traditional atmosphere away from the beach activities, try the **Santa Catalina**, in Parque Doramas (tel: 24 30 40). It is surrounded by tall, cool palms in beautiful gardens. The hotel also boasts the only casino in Las Palmas.

Nearer the old town, the 4-star **Melia Confort Iberia** (tel: 36 11 33) on Avenida Marítima del Norte is a good, functional, businesslike hotel which is also extremely comfortable.

Maspalomas area
Barbacan Sol, Avenida Tirajana 25, Playa del Inglés (tel: 77 20 30). Comfortable, well-appointed hotel with apartments built round garden and swimming pool. Each apartment has its own terrace, cooking and dining facilities. Excellent Basque cuisine in hotel dining-room.
Faro Maspalomas, Plaza del Faro, (tel: 14 22 14). A beautifully positioned hotel with glorious sea views and a fantastic restaurant that's one of the best of the island.

Conventional hotels that do not provide apartment accommodation are often in the luxury class:
Meliá Taramindos, Calle Retama 3, San Agustín (tel: 77 40 90). Famous for its casino and cabaret floor show. Breakfast can be taken on the terrace, buffet lunch by the pool, and dinner in the grand dining-room. The hotel's beautiful gardens lead straight on to the beach.
Maspalomas Oasis, Maspalomas beach (tel: 14 14 48). On the southernmost tip of the island near the lighthouse, this is *the* luxury hotel of Maspalomas. It has everything, including Julio Iglesias as one of its frequent guests.

Puerto Rico
The accommodation here is mostly apartment hotels. There are children's pools in most hotels, and excursions laid on by hotels often include supervised day-trips to places of interest.
Courtesy buses run every half-hour for those at the top of the hill who want to come down to the beach.

Camping
There are two official sites on the island:
Guantánamo, Playa Tauro (tel: 56 02 07). Just west of Puerto Rico. Good shade down to the sea, with an annexe on the other side of the road.
Temisas, Lomo de la Cruz (tel: 79 81 49). Travelling south from the airport, come off at the Arinaga intersection. Eight miles (12km) from the beach of Arinage but a beautiful, rural site.

Children
Most hotels in the south have a children's pool and entertainment programme. There are also bowling alleys and amusement arcades, roller-skating and mini-golf away from the beach. In Maspalomas, **Ocean Park** provides well-supervised water slides, pools and fountains, and a huge fairground during the school holidays with all manner of rides and stalls. **Sioux City** near San Agustín stages popular Wild West shows.

Culture, Entertainment and Nightlife
Las Palmas
The **Opera Festival** is held from the beginning of February to mid-March. Singers like

Montserrat Caballé, Luciano Pavarotti and Plácido Domingo perform here. The **Philharmonic Orchestra** of Gran Canaria is in residence at the Teatro Pérez Galdos, Lentini 1, from the beginning of October to the middle of June. The **Spring Festival of Music and Dance** in April/May also commands internationally known guest performers. Nightlife and entertainment is something you do not have to search for in Las Palmas. It is everywhere, particularly in the Canteras and the Santa Catalina park area. The large hotels always have something going on and they can offer some terrific entertainment. Try **Dino's** on the top of Los Bardinos hotel, **Zorba's** on Luis Morote and **Toca Toca** on Plaza de España are recommended for young disco enthusiasts; **Utopia** pub on Calle Tomás Miller is a lively place for any age. Louder, earthier places exist, of course, and can be found with no difficulty.

In the Maspalomas area, the casino at the **Meliá Taramindos Hotel**, San Agustín, is very popular with those who want to inject a bit of risk into their lives. You can also order a proper meal, as opposed to a snack, in the early hours of the morning. The **Son a Mar** floorshow is a great attraction. All pink, with polished floors and lights and mirrors, seating 1,000 people to watch the dancing girls as well as top class cabaret and variety acts (smart dress required). Most of the popular entertainment can be found in Playa del Inglés, and people from other resorts will come here for a lively nightlife.

The **Metro** precinct has folk-singing and dancing on Sunday mornings. Discos are everywhere, but the most popular include **Joy**, **Pachá** and **Terraza El Metro**, all three in Playa del Inglés, and **Beach Club** and **Gramófono** in San Agustín.

Restaurants
Las Palmas
Casa Julio, Calle La Naval 132 (tel: 46 01 39), in the port area, is universally acknowledged as the best fish restaurant in Las Palmas. Not a pretentious place but excellent food.
El Novillo Precoz, Calle Portugal 9 (tel: 22 16 59), just behind the Playa del las Canteras. Substantial portions of meat, well cooked over wood fires in the Argentinean manner. For a Thai meal, try **Bangkok Beach** which overlooks the beach at Las Canteras (tel: 26 46 03) or Chinese, at **Chino House Ming** at Luis Morote 56, near the Santa Catalina Park (tel: 27 45 63). For Austrian food, try **Asturias** at Calle Miguel Rosas 5 (tel: 27 42 19). At **Pasta Real**, Calle Secretario Padilla 28, (tel: 26 22 67) there is a choice of pasta, macrobiotic and vegetarian dishes. Delicious Galician seafood is served at **Meson Condado**, Ferreras 22 (tel: 46 94 43). For sheer luxury, it would be difficult to beat the **Parrilla Reina Isabel,** the restaurant of the 5-star hotel of the same name, Calle Alfredo L Jones 40 (tel: 26 01 00).

Playa del Inglés
The variety of restaurants in this resort is enormous but

Folk dancing at the Pueblo Canario in Las Palmas

most fall into the cheap and cheerful category.
Rias Bajas on the Avenida . Norteamerica displays loud advertisements outside but the atmosphere inside is much more restrained. Excellent Galician menu and a tapas bar as well. **La Toja**, another Galician restaurant, is on the Avenida Tirajana (tel: 76 11 96); in this road too is fresh Italian food at **La Liguria**. The hot bread alone is worth the visit. **La Casa Vieja**, on Carretera a Fataga, is always full of locals which is a good sign. **Bali**, on Avenida Tirajana (tel: 76 32 61) is an Indonesian restaurant much patronised by Dutch visitors.

San Agustín
The **Beach Club** at Playa de los Cocoteros (tel: 76 04 00) has an excellent restaurant serving international food by the poolside. Pleasant, elegant atmosphere. The Italian **Chez Mario** restaurant at the *urbanización* Nueva Europa (tel: 76 18 17) is less expensive and very agreeable.

Shopping
Since the days after 1852 when the island ports were declared free with no restrictions on trade and no payment of duty, **Las Palmas** in particular has been known as a shopper's paradise. There are two main shopping centres – the pedestrianised street of **Mayor de Triana** in the south near the old town and the **Avenida de Mesa y López** near the port to the north. **Maya** is the prestigious department store in the old town and **El Corte Inglés** in the new. There are numerous bazaars, shops owned by Indian traders whose families came to the island in the last century and who now deal largely in **electronic equipment**. You will find a good selection of these shops in the streets north and west of **Santa Catalina Park** and in the **Calle Juan Rejón** by the Castillo de la Luz. Be sceptical of signs advertising a closing down sale or final reductions; and certainly prepare to bargain. You should remember the duty you may have to pay to take goods back home before you agree a final price, and make sure you know precisely what you are buying. Clever copies of expensive brand names abound. The open stalls in **Santa**

Catalina Park sell inexpensive clothes, badly cured leather goods and tourist souvenirs. Las Palmas also has a morning *rastro* or **flea market** on Sundays on the Avenida Maritimo. There is a **food market** by López Socas and Rosarito in the port area and one between Néstor de la Torre and Barcelona immediately south of Mesa y López. The oldest one is on the edge of the Old Town on the corner of **Calle Mendizabal**. In the Playa del Inglés area, there are several huge **shopping/eating/ entertainment precincts** open all through the evening. For those who prefer to shop where Canarians go, there is the market on Wednesday mornings and Saturdays at **San Fernando**, the local residential area immediately west of the Playa del Inglés.

For **local craft work**, like basket weaving and embroidery, go to the town of Ingenio, southwest of the airport. Here you can watch the work in progress before you buy anything. The *timple*, a five-stringed Canarian musical instrument, is made at Telde and there is a pottery at Arucas. For a shop selling Canarian craft goods, try the **Artesania Canaria Taguguy** at Calle Armas in the Vegueta district of Las Palmas.

Special Events

Local supporters say that the **Las Palmas and Maspalomas Carnival** (February/March) is second only to Rio de Janeiro – a claim also made on behalf of Santa Cruz de Tenerife. Lots of dancing and not much sleep.

There are many local festivals and celebrations like the **Bajada de Rama**, the Descent of the Branch, at Agaete on 4 August. (See Agaete, **What To See**, above.) Carpets of flowers mark **Corpus Christi** in June in Las Palmas and Arucas.

Sport
Las Palmas
Surfing and windsurfing: beyond the natural barrier reef on Bahía del Confital. **Sailing**: from the two marinas of Puerto Deportivo, Calle León y Castillo and the Real Club Náutico de Gran Canaria at Puerto de la Luz. **Deep-sea fishing**: excursions from Santa Catalina Pier in the port leave every day at noon. **Tennis**: at El Tenis Centre, Maspalomas, with its 11 clay courts and professional help if required(tel: 76 74 47) and the Club Náutico Metropole, Paseo Alonoso Quesada (tel: 24 43 46), where there are also **swimming pools** and **squash courts**. **Golf** is a major sport on Gran Canaria. Closest course to Las Palmas is the Bandama Club (18-hole course), 9 miles (14km) from Las Palmas on the Carretera del Centro. You can also go **horse-riding** here. **Greyhound racing**: at Campo España dogtrack in Calle Obispo Romo.

Cock fights take place in the López Socas Stadium from December to May. At the same stadium you can see **Canarian wrestling** (*lucha Canaraia*). Typical Canarian-style sailing boats are *lateens*, small with large sails. See them Saturday afternoon and Sunday morning from April to September along

THE EASTERN ISLANDS – GRAN CANARIA

The magnificent Golf Club de Bandama is the oldest in all of Spain and her territories

the Avenida Marítima.

Maspalomas area

A variety of watersports are available in most resorts; sailing, windsurfing, scuba diving and so on. Apply to your hotel for information or contact Sun Club, Playa del Inglés (tel: 76 28 70) or Inter Club Atlantic, San Agustín (tel: 76 09 50).

Most hotels of any size provide **tennis** courts.

At Real Aero Club de Gran Canaria (tel: 15 71 47), you can hire light **aircraft** or go **parachuting**, **sky diving** and **free falling**. If starting from scratch it takes 3–4 months to get a pilot's licence. There is a parachuting course with soft landings on Maspalomas sand dunes. The **go-kart track** is great fun, for youngsters and adults, and is claimed to be the largest in Spain (1,312 yards/1,200m). The Campo de Golf de Maspalomas, Avda Neckerman (tel: 76 25 81) is an excellent 18-hole, par 72 course, and the main reason why many **golf** enthusiasts come to this resort. **Horse-riding** and riding lessons for the more serious are available at Picadero del Oasis, (tel: 76 23 78).

Or try a **camel safari** through the sand dunes: the address is Carretera del Faro de Maspalomas.

Puerto Rico

Renowned **watersports** facilities. Contact the sailing school – Escuela Territorial de Vela de Puerta Rico, Calle Doreste (tel: 56 07 72).

FUERTEVENTURA

General Information

Size: 688 square miles (1,731sq km). Largest of the Canary Islands after Tenerife, but most thinly populated – 30,000.
68 miles (110km) at its longest point and 19 miles (30km) at its widest.
Highest point: Orejas de Asno 2,648 feet (807m).

For modern visitors the attraction is the beach – miles of glorious clean white sand stretching as far as the eye can see, with small protected bays, crests of sand like mountain ridges, and golden peaks that shelve into a bright blue sea. After that comes wind, tearing out of an equally blue sky and often threatening the pleasures of the beach. When windiest, however, Fuerteventura is a windsurfer's paradise, one of the world's leading spots for speed sailing, with possibilities for spectacular aqua-gymnastics and, in places, plain, honest-to-goodness surfing.
So far, there are relatively few visitors to Fuerteventura, at least compared to neighbouring Lanzarote. They come in two contrasting types – seekers of peace and quiet on one hand and, on the other, the young and super-fit, clad in surfers' polychrome gear.
The island itself is extraordinary, stark and bare to the point of desperation, wind-buffeted and almost waterless. To some, aside from beach and watersports, it seems entirely charmless, well symbolised by the fact that this is the last outpost of the Spanish Foreign Legion. However, the Legion's few barracks are one of the features of the dull, modern capital, Puerto del Rosario.
To others, Fuerteventura is an inspiration, with grandeur in the very bareness and splendour of evening skies that throw huge patterns of cerise and mauve across the forbidding mountains. The great Spanish philosopher, Miguel de Unamuno, exiled here in the 1920s, described the island as 'an oasis in the desert of civilisation'.
The sand-dunes, unquestionably beautiful, are in the north near Corralejo and along the Jandía peninsula in the south. These are the island's two major

A mill harvests Fuerteventura's main commodity – the wind

THE EASTERN ISLANDS – FUERTEVENTURA

resorts. Between, there lies a handful of sights which are worth visiting, but extremely few by comparison with any other of the Canary Islands. This is a large island and parts of it remain rugged, inaccessible and scarcely tamed.

Island History

Arriving in 1405 to claim the island for Spain, Jean de Béthencourt is said to have remarked 'What a great adventure', '*Que fuerte ventura*'. Or perhaps it was the strong wind, *el viento fuerte* which gave the island its name. Betancuria, in the mountains of the west, is named after the conqueror. Having overcome two separate tribes of indigenous inhabitants, Béthencourt brought in settlers from Normandy and Spain. In the early days the island was more fertile and there was a considerable trade in goat hides. Apart from that, there is little to report from many centuries of hard slog. World War II, however, brought a hint of drama. Franco's Spain, though neutral in the conflict, inclined politically towards Germany. Large and guarded private German land holdings in the south of Fuerteventura brought inevitable rumours of submarine activity and it is widely believed that some war criminals made their escape to Latin America from this coast. Tourism came late to Fuerteventura but now shows signs of pulling the island, sometimes reluctantly, into the last years of the 20th century.

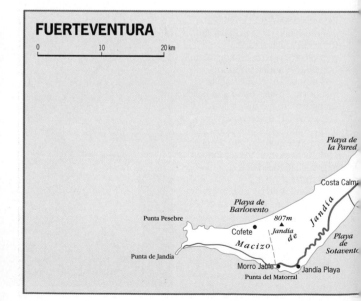

FUERTEVENTURA

0   10   20 km

Playa de la Pared

Costa Calma

Jandía

Playa de Barlovento

Punta Pesebre

807m

Cofete   *Jandía de*

Macizo

Playa de Sotavento

Punta de Jandía

Morro Jable   Jandía Playa

Punta del Matorral

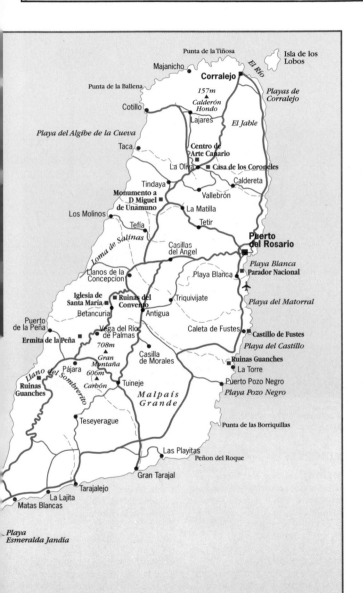

Fuerteventura may be stark and bare, but it does have a certain grandeur

RESORTS

The main resorts, Corralejo and Jandía, are compact, not to say dense, and are positioned to take advantage of the best beaches. Corralejo is favoured by the British and Jandía by the Germans. Other spots, some of them decidedly less promising, have recently begun a rapid development, providing a surge of time-share and apartment possibilities.

◆◆
CALETA DE FUSTES/EL CASTILLO

6 miles (10km) south of airport
This resort on the east coast is a sudden low-rise eruption on either side of a main road passing through a low-lying plain. Tucked immediately around the village's little castle and adjacent harbour, there is a pleasant complex – **Club el Castillo** – with swimming pool, apartments, shops, restaurants and bars. The golden, sandy beach is safe and well protected, good for children.

CORRALEJO

23 miles (38km) north of airport
Corralejo and Playas de
Corralejo, on the northeast tip
of the island, effectively make
up a single resort which is
popular with British and
German visitors. At Playas de
Corralejo two large hotels are
sited at the northern end of the
6-mile (10km) beach right on
the sand. The beach itself is
backed by a system of romantic
and beautiful sand dunes. The
two big hotels, the Riu Palace
Tres Islas and Riu Oliva Beach,
are something of an
environmental disaster; but for
those who stay in them, their
position is a source of delight.
Now, somewhat late in the
day, the dunes have finally
achieved legal protection.
From the two big hotels, new
apartments stretch north almost
to Corralejo village.
Corralejo proper was formerly
centred on its small market
square and harbour. Now a
newly built commercial centre,
the Centro Atlantico, with shops
and restaurants, has moved the
focus further down into the long
main street. From Corralejo
there are frequent ferry
crossings to Lanzarote, just
across the straits and a boat
takes day trippers to the tiny
island of Los Lobos (see **What
to See**, below).

◆◆
JANDÍA
Jandía is the general name
applied to the strip of holiday
development running north
from Morro del Jable along the
Jandía peninsula almost to

Tarajalejo. It owes its position to
the Playa de Sotavento, a vast
beach running northwards from
Morro del Jable. The village of
Morro del Jable sits on either
side of an old river-bed, with a
school, a football pitch and
one main shopping street that
leads down to the sea. This
represents the older, more
settled life of local people. The
new life is represented by the
busy line of bars and
restaurants along the beach and
just behind, and by the new
apartments and chalets.
Jandía itself is growing fast,
mostly with apartment hotels,
commercial centres and
restaurants. All along the road
towards the southern end of the
peninsula, deep in gullies and
high on knobs of hill, there are
also new developments, or
'urbanisations', of identical
white houses ranged in serried
ranks. The scenery northwards
from the resort is generally
gaunt, but well below the road,
reached by rough tracks
downwards, there lies the
glorious fringe of beach. This
varies in width and is protected
in places by a sand-bar, creating
a lagoon-like effect. Along the
whole of its length it is golden,
brilliant and often empty.

PUERTO DEL ROSARIO

Despite its capital status there is
nothing in this town to detain
tourists. If you have time to kill
while waiting for a ferry here,
take a look at the small garden
in front of the Foreign Legion
headquarters (see below). The
parador just outside town is a
pleasant place to spend a night.

The Spanish Foreign Legion
While Spain still clings onto her North African territories of Ceuta and Melilla, it's likely that Fuerteventura, the nearest Canarian territory to Africa, will remain the base for that most hard-bitten of all its armed forces – the Spanish Foreign Legion. Their headquarters is in Puerto del Rosario, on the Corralejo road next to the port. Here, in formal gardens in front of the barracks, is a display of modern weaponry, heroic statues and some curious wooden totem poles.

WHAT TO SEE ON FUERTEVENTURA

BETANCURIA
30 miles (48km) south of Corralejo
Founded by Jean de Béthencourt in 1405, this town was the capital of the island until 1834. Though tiny and somewhat decrepit, it has a serious and settled look, as monumental as this island gets. The site was chosen for its fertility and for its inaccessibility. It proved, in the end, not inaccessible enough.

Iglesia de Santa María
The church, originally a cathedral, was founded by Béthencourt and destroyed by pirates in 1539. Slowly rebuilt, it now has an 18th-century air. The interior is simple, broad and open. The gilded high altar dates from the second half of the 17th century and the ceiling has decorated beams, very typical of the Canaries.

Museo de Arte Sacro
In the basement of a building which doubles up as home of the curate, the Sacred Art Museum houses an interesting collection of photographs of all the island churches as well as vestments, carvings, and other works of art.

Other public buildings in Betancuria include the small **Museo Arqueológico** (Archaeological Museum) on the far side of the gully from the former cathedral (*open*: Tuesday to Saturday 10.00–17.00hrs, Sunday 10.00–14.00hrs) and a roofless and ruined **Franciscan friary** to the north of the town. South of Betancuria, villages nestle in deep valleys in the most handsome landscapes of the island.

ISLA DE LOS LOBOS
This tiny island, just under 2 miles (3km) off the coast of Fuerteventura, is reached by glass-bottomed boat and a converted fishing boat from Corralejo. Guided parties take picnics and barbecues. It offers good swimming, exceptionally fine views and hardly a scrap of shade. Depending on sea and wind, the northwest corner of the island provides terrifying-looking surfing for the brave and experienced.

LA OLIVA
10 miles (16km) south of Corralejo
The main administrative centre of the north of the island and, until the 19th century, its military

base. The **Casa de los Coroneles** (House of the Colonels) dating from the 18th century, stands at the outskirts of the village. It was the grand home of the military commander of the island and now stands empty, a romantic ruin. The house is cream coloured, with an enormous black stone armorial doorway and florid woodwork balconies looking like the last crumbling defiance of the desert. The other substantial building in the village is the 18th-century parish church which holds some fine paintings, but is currently undergoing lengthy restoration work. Very definitely open is the new **Centro de Arte Canario**, one of the finest collections of

Betancuria is the historic heart of Fuerteventura

modern Canarian art on the islands. Works range from completely avant-garde to completely accessible and are well displayed in traditional and modern settings.

◆
PÁJARA
9 miles (15km) south of Betancuria
After Betancuria, this is the prettiest village on the island of Fuerteventura, shady, floral and well ordered. The most attractive building is the church. Its portals are framed in Aztec-influenced statuary of rosettes with animals breathing fire out of wide open mouths. The interior of the church is charming, with a coffered ceiling and the altar screens in each of the two aisles prettily painted in simple, floral style.

Accommodation
Corralejo

Corralejo town has mostly small purpose-built houses and apartments bookable through tour operators. Corralejo Playa has two major beach hotels: **Riu Palace Tres Islas**, 5-star (tel: 53 57 00). Very comfortable, with most of the facilities of a 5-star hotel – air conditioning, pool, tennis courts and a full entertainment programme. Smooth, smart service.
Riu Oliva Beach, 3-star (tel: 86 61 00). A comfortable, well-placed family hotel with small rooms but an exceptional situation on the edge of the dunes. There is a swimming and sunbathing area, and an all day children's club.

Jandía

Los Gorriones Sol, 3-star (tel: 54 70 25) is north of the resort, in a beautiful, isolated situation right on Sotavento beach with two pools, sun terraces, and gardens. Windsurf facilities and tuition are available from the F2 windsurfing school at the hotel.

Puerto del Rosario/Playa Barca

Parador de Fuerteventura, 3-star, Playa Blanca (just south of Puerto del Rosario) (tel: 85 11 50). State-run hotel on a rather grim, grey beach, much used by local lads surfing. The *parador* looks like an army barracks from the outside, but bears the customary trademarks of *parador* style inside – comfort and quality.

Restaurants
Corralejo

El Corsraio serves local dishes such as Manchengo cheese and churros de pescado (fried fish). Spanish music plays and there's a lovely wood-covered street terrace with tables. Hawaiian cocktail bar, **Marquesina** is a good place for lunch, used by locals as well as tourists. Sit outside by the small fishing harbour and watch the windsurfers zipping about. **Riu Palace Tres Islas Hotel** (tel: 53 57 00). À la carte menu offers an excellent choice of international and Spanish food. Elegant surroundings and good service.

Jandía

Choice is plentiful. **La Goleta** is fitted out like a ship's saloon with a lot of brass and rope and wood. Multi-lingual menus and very popular.
Saavedra has great atmosphere, and serves up authentic Spanish food. Located downstairs in the commercial centre.

Entertainment and Nightlife

Evening entertainments are usually available in the large hotels. There are some discos in Jandía and Corralejo but Fuerteventura is not the place for a lively night life.

Shopping

Not a leading activity on Fuerteventura. Shops in the commercial precincts of **Corralejo** and **Jandía** resorts have the greatest variety of consumer goods, from electronic equipment to designer swimwear. The larger hotels also have boutiques. At the village of **Lajares** between Cotillo and La Oliva, the **lace** and **embroidery** workshop offers its wares. Self-caterers will find all they need at **Hiperfuer** in Puerto del Carmen.

Beaches and climate make Fuerteventura one of the world's best windsurfing centres

Special Events

Each little hamlet has its own saint's day festival but on the third Saturday in September everybody celebrates the **Fiesta de la Virgen de la Peña**, the feast of the patroness of the island. There is a general pilgrimage to Vega del Río de Palmas near Betancuria.

Sport

Caleta de Fustes/El Castillo provides ideal facilities for beginners to **windsurfing** and **scuba diving**.

Corralejo has rather more rigorous conditions for **windsurfing**, **scuba diving** and **mountain biking**; also **surfing** expeditions to Isla de Lobos, but only for the brave. Contact the Trade Winds Centre. Tres Islas and Oliva Beach hotels also organise **diving** lessons one day a week.

Cotillo and the beaches south of the little harbour are where the **wave sailing** enthusiasts spend their days.

Jandía, and Los Corriones Hotel in particular, is the home of the F2 windsurfing school. Here, off Sotovento Beach, is where speed surfers try to break world records.

LANZAROTE

General Information
Size: 307 square miles (795sq km). 37 miles (60km) from north to south, 12½ miles (20km) at its widest.
Highest point Peñas del Chache, 2,214 feet (675m).
Population: 80,000.

'Magical' and 'mysterious' are words often used to describe Lanzarote. They carry a hint that there is something more to this island than the beautiful sandy beaches and sunshine that it enjoys in abundance. Like the rest of the Canaries, it has all the characteristics of land blown up from the sea bed in explosions of fire and boiling lava. But here, the volcanic upheavals and the ingenious methods by which the people have survived them have left a landscape that is not just extraordinary but positively startling.

The Timanfaya National Park is now a place for tourists to gasp at, but the eruptions in the 18th century that produced the Montañas del Fuego (Mountains of Fire) were a disaster for the islanders. Nearly a quarter of the most fertile surface of the island was submerged under 20–35 feet (6–10m) of lava. Many people had no alternative but to leave the island.

The volcanic rock from these former scenes of devastation comes in all colours, shapes, textures and sizes. There are black, red and grey craters, fields of jagged rocks as high as a man, grey rubble, and, in places, a rich volcanic soil which supports an astonishingly varied

LANZAROTE

0   5   10 km

El Volcá

Parque

Islot
de Hilari
Nacional de
Montaña
del Fuego

Timanfaya

El Golfo
El Golfo

Echadero de
los Camellos ■
(Camel Park)

Los
Hervideros

Yaiza

Salinas ■
de Janubio

Las Hoyas

Punta
Ginés

Femés

El Rubicon

Playa
Blanca

Castillo de
las Coloradas

Punta de
Pechiguera

Playas
Papagayo

Punta de
Papagayo

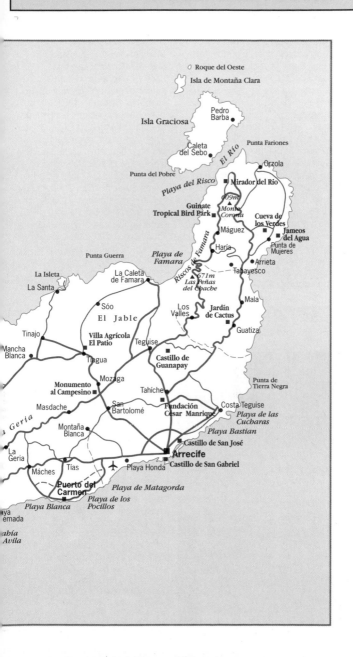

THE EASTERN ISLANDS – LANZAROTE

agriculture. The natural vegetation is sparse and as for trees, there are none, except palms and tamarisk.

The people live in small settlements of white houses with beautiful onion-domed chimney stacks and tidy gardens which look like car parks, covered as they are in black volcanic soil. The villages are scattered over the island wherever a living can be made out of the soil. To the north the land rises fast, then falls in sudden steep cliffs to the sea, with the islands of Graciosa, Montaña Clara and Alegranza lying straight ahead. The west coast, which includes the Timanfaya national park, is wild and rugged. The major tourist

The intense heat of the 'Mountains of Fire' is demonstrated when water is transformed into a scalding geyser

resorts lie on the eastern side of the island where the land shelves down gently into sandy beaches and coves running much of the way along to the southernmost point. From here it is just 40 minutes by ferry to Fuerteventura.

The tourist resorts are in their way as surprising as the villages. There are none of the concrete towers which characterise so many other holiday destinations, no advertisement hoardings, or electricity pylons. Having entered the tourist market later than some of the other islands, Lanzarote has learned from their mistakes. Developers strain to bend the rules governing the size and appearance of any new building, however, and sometimes succeed.

Construction now underway in the south and round the main resort of Puerto del Carmen is in places far too dense. But in general, and certainly in comparison to Gran Canaria and Tenerife, tourism is not yet spoiling the island.

César Manrique

The man chiefly responsible for this happy state was the late César Manrique, artist, designer, sculptor and architect of international standing. He was born on the island and strove to ensure that all new building, however modern in concept, should share the simple elegance of traditional architecture, and be in harmony with its singular volcanic landscape. The visitor arriving at the airport can see precisely what he meant. The interior of the airport was designed by Manrique.

THE EASTERN ISLANDS – LANZAROTE

Outside the resort areas, most people still make their living from agriculture and fishing. This, on an island with virtually no rainfall, is an achievement. The northeast trade winds bring rain to the more mountainous islands and sweep dryly over Lanzarote's low hills. The farmers, though, have discovered that the porous lava granules in which their crops are grown store the moisture of the evening dew and release it slowly during the day, as well as providing a barrier against wind and sun. So the very lava that once destroyed their living is now used to restore it. Hence the asphalt look of many fields and gardens.

This method is used to produce Lanzarote's Malvasia wine (or Malmsey) for the export market. The islanders grow onions, tomatoes, watermelon, squash, potatoes, cereals, corn and tobacco. Cochineal, a food and cosmetic colouring produced by beetles reared on prickly pear plants, is still an important export despite the modern use of aniline dyes. Fishing also plays an important part in the island economy. The waters between Lanzarote and the African coast are rich fishing grounds and Arrecife is the home of the largest fishing fleet in the Canaries.

At 80,000, the population is small but growing. Despite the arrival of tourism most inhabitants of Lanzarote remain rooted in a traditional, rural culture with a distinct and vigorous life of its own. Visitors to the island each year number over one million. Most of these restrict themselves to the small tourist enclaves on the coast. All the more room,

then, for those who want a more enriching experience of Lanzarote, to explore the unspoilt countryside and meet the people.

Island History

The first recorded contact with Europe occurred in 1312 with the arrival of the Genoese sailor, Lancelloti Malocello. It is likely that he gave his name to the island. In 1402 the Norman adventurers Gadifer de la Salle and Jean de Béthencourt took the island in the name of the Spanish crown and used it as a base from which to mount expeditions against other islands in the group. When these had all been subdued, Lanzarote was left largely to its own devices and the mercies of French, English, Dutch and Arab slaving pirates. Their constant attentions explain the siting of the old capital, Teguise, right in the centre of the island, and the presence today of towers and fortifications along the coast. Up to 1837, Lanzarote remained a fiefdom of the Spanish crown. In 1730, a series of huge volcanic explosions occurred in the western part of the island. These eruptions continued for six years, destroying 77 square miles (200sq km) of the most fertile land in the island. By 1736, a third of the island was covered with a layer of lava 33 feet (10m) thick, burying 11 villages beneath it. More eruptions occurred in 1824 bringing the number of volcanoes to 29. Timanfaya is the highest crater at 1,673 feet (510m) and gives its name to the national park.

An upheaval of another sort has been the great increase in

tourist traffic to the island in the last twenty years. Visitors are mostly from Germany, the United Kingdom, Scandinavia and mainland Spain. The presence of so many people has helped to create water shortages, and there are frequent requests to be sparing in its use. Care is required, even with modern desalination plants.

RESORTS

◆
COSTA TEGUISE
4 miles (7km) northeast of Arrecife
This large, new, up-market *urbanización* (development) is built around an excellent sandy beach. Watersport facilities are good and there is an 18-hole golf course and aquapark on site. Development generally obeys the rules laid down for the island by César Manrique – low-rise buildings, with green, blue or brown paintwork. But the further away from the smartest part, the more the resort sprawls into unfinished *urbanizaciones* with apartments only half full and empty shopping precincts to let. There are several bars, restaurants and supermarkets to cater for the needs of holiday-makers, but Costa Teguise will never be as crowded as Puerto del Carmen, nor as animated.

◆◆◆
PLAYA BLANCA
Originally a small fishing village in the southwestern end of the island, its periphery is rapidly being transformed by more and more tourist building – hotels, apartments and apartment hotels, many of them at some

Picturesque Puerto del Carmen is Lanzarote's most popular resort

distance from any beach. The area immediately behind the small, sandy beach in the middle of town retains a pleasant atmosphere, with bars and restaurants on the promenade. There is a marina for pleasure craft as well as a busy quay for the ferry to Fuerteventura. An eastwards turn outside Playa Blanca directs you to the Papagayo beaches. From here there are no further signs, just a maze of bumpy, dusty tracks which lead to the most stunning

and uncrowded beaches on the island; Playa de Mujeres, Playa Papagayo, Puerto Muelas (La Caleta).

◆◆◆
PUERTO DEL CARMEN
the Old Town is 6 miles (10km) southwest of the airport
This little harbour settlement just south of Arrecife has expanded northwards along a series of beaches to become one of the major resorts of the Canary Islands. The majority of holiday-makers on the island are based here. There are some larger hotels on the beach near the town but much tourist accommodation is found behind the numerous small-scale shopping centres, locally known as *arcades*, which run almost the length of the Avenida de las Playas. The arcades have shops, restaurants, pubs, discos and snack-bars by the score. But though it is sprawling, populous and cheerful, there are no high-rise buildings at all and the atmosphere is considerably calmer than at comparable resorts on the other islands. The beaches all merge into one 5-mile (8km) stretch of sand but it is convenient to distinguish

between different stretches. The first, going west from the harbour in the direction of the airport, is now known as **Playa Blanca**. It is the nearest beach to the centre of town, the most popular and the most crowded. The next beach, **Los Pocillos**, is much quieter, largely used by locals at the weekends. Here the large hotels begin again and there is less impression of a busy, holiday-makers' seafront. The old part of town survives around the picturesque fishing port. This is a charming, small area of good fish restaurants and down-to-earth bars where old sea-dogs and tourists rub shoulders. In the square next to the port you can watch the locals playing *boules*.

ARRECIFE

Arrecife has been the capital city of the island since 1852 and is the home of more than half the population. It is also the only place in Lanzarote where you will experience a traffic jam. This busy commercial centre is built round a couple of harbours protected by extensive offshore reefs – 'arrecife' means 'reef'. The harbour to the north, Puerto de la Naos, is where the really serious business of fishing and fish processing happens. The promenade along the sea front is planted with attractive gardens. Arrecife is not old and its historic buildings are few. But it does have one interesting natural feature – a lagoon, Charco de San Ginés. This hardly makes Arrecife the 'Venice of the Atlantic', as some writers of tourist literature like to

have it, but the lagoon, known to locals as 'The Puddle', is bordered by restaurants and shops in an attractive setting.

WHAT TO SEE IN ARRECIFE

CASTILLO DE SAN GABRIEL

The castle is on a tiny offshore island reached by either a road bridge or an older foot-bridge. At the centre of the latter is a tiny drawbridge called the Puente de las Bolas or Bridge of the Balls (there are two cannon balls on top of columns). The fortress was built in 1590 by the Italian architect Leonardo Torriani to defend the town from pirate raids. Now it serves as a small archaeological museum. *Open*: Monday to Friday 08.00–14.00hrs.

CASTILLO DE SAN JOSÉ/ MUSEO INTERNACIONAL DE ARTE CONTEMPORÁNEO

Beyond the deep-water fishing port at the north end of town, this little castle was built in the 18th century on the orders of King Philip II, to provide work for the islanders. Once built, it was used as a munitions store. Its present and more noble function is as the International Museum of Contemporary Art, the brain child of the Lanzarote artist and architect, César Manrique. He rescued it from dereliction in the 1960s and with a grant from the government began to buy important contemporary works. You will find paintings and sculptures by Picasso and Miró, and by César Manrique himself

A short causeway links the centre of Arrecife to the Castillo de San Gabriel

here, beautifully lit and displayed against a background of dark volcanic walls. Below the museum, a restaurant, also designed by Manrique, offers sweeping views of the harbour entrance and the sea.
Museum open: daily, 11.00–21.00hrs.

◆
IGLESIA DE SAN GINÉS
The church of the patron saint of the island is not particularly grand but, like all Canarian churches, it is well proportioned. It has a lovely Moorish-style (*artesanado*) ceiling. Like many Canarian churches, it is in the middle of restoration after long years of neglect. It stands with its back to the lagoon of

San Ginés, at one end of a square where old men sit on shady benches.
Open: daily 09.00–13.00hrs, 17.00–19.00hrs

WHAT TO SEE OUTSIDE ARRECIFE

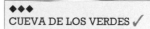
◆◆◆
CUEVA DE LOS VERDES ✓

A network of underground tunnels and caves at the foot of the Corona volcano which connects with those at the Jameos del Agua (see below), to the northeast of the caves. The guide takes you on a half-mile (1km) trip through atmospherically lit tunnels and caves created by the eruption of the Corona volcano. The outside crust of the rivers of molten lava cooled and solidified while the boiling mass inside continued its

way on downwards to the sea,
leaving hollow passages where
it flowed out. Through the
centuries, they have been a
place of refuge for islanders
against pirate attack. Today the
caves are one of the island's
prime tourist attractions. The
highlight of the tour comes at the
very end with a brilliant natural
optical illusion (to describe it is
to destroy it!), which in itself is
worth the admission fee.
Tours daily, on the hour, 10.00–
18.00hrs (last tour 17.00hrs).

◆◆
EL GOLFO
8 miles (12km) northwest of Yaiza
This is a lagoon of deep emerald
green in the rim of half a
volcanic crater, the other half of

*Haría is a traditional summer
retreat for islanders*

which is submerged in the sea.
It is on the western edge of
Timanfaya National Park, and
steep cliffs of black, red and
grey offer a startling contrast with
the bright green of the lagoon.
The intensity of colour is caused
by the effects of algae in the
water. Due to evaporation, the
salt content of the water is highly
concentrated. From the lagoon,
a black, gravely beach shelves
steeply down to the ocean.

◆◆◆
FUNDACIÓN CÉSAR MANRIQUE
*Tahiche, 4 miles (6km) north of
Arrecife*
The home and studio of the
famous Lanzarote artist César
Manrique, was opened to the
public in 1992 after his death. It
houses a collection of his own
paintings and sculptures. The

lower part of the house has been built into an ancient lava bed. The cave-like rooms are actually volcanic bubbles created by the eruptions of 1730–36.
Open: November to June, Monday to Saturday 10.00–18.00hrs; July to October daily, 10.00–19.00hrs.

HARÍA
9 miles (15km) northeast of Teguise
A pretty, white village set in 'a valley of a thousand palms', and a source of great pride for people who are all too aware of the lack of trees on the island. With its low white houses scattered in the cool green valley Haría has the look of a North African town, and traditionally it has been a popular place for islanders to retreat to in the summer. Two-and-a-half miles (4km) south of the village a *mirador* offers marvellous views of the valley of Tabayesco below.

ISLA GRACIOSA
There is a crossing from Orzola on the north of Lanzarote to Caleta del Sabo each morning and afternoon in the season, according to demand. The island has no tarred roads, no cars and no shade. But it does have wonderful empty beaches and sand dunes and, at the small fishing village of Caleta del Sabo, food, drink and a pension.

◆◆◆
JAMEOS DEL AGUA
17 miles (27km) north of Arrecife
The same lava stream which

created the Cueva de los Verdes finally met the waters of the Atlantic at this point, one mile (2km) away. And at this most improbable juncture, César Manrique has created an underground complex of lagoon/ restaurant/nightclub/tropical garden and swimming pool. A wooden staircase leads down to a large underground cave with an opening to the sky which barely provides enough light to reveal the small sea water lagoon at your feet. The floor of the lagoon is dotted with white specks – blind white crabs that were stranded here long ago, usually only found in the ocean at depths of below 10,000 feet (3,000m). Steps then ascend to emerge back into the brilliant sunshine and palm trees of a rocky tropical garden.
Open: Jul–Sep, daily 09.30–19.00hrs; Oct–Jun, daily 11.00–18.45hrs, also Tuesday, Friday and Saturday 19.00–03.00hrs (folklore show at 23.00hrs).

◆◆
JARDIN DE CACTUS
Guatiza, 11 miles (17km) northeast of Arrecife
Don't be put off by the dry-sounding concept of a cactus garden. This is an inspired piece of landscaping with over 10,000 specimens of all shapes and sizes, interspersed with huge finger-shaped volcanic rocks, reminiscent of a Dalí painting. The centrepiece is a beautifully preserved windmill which still grinds *gofio* (see page 113).
Open: Summer, daily, 10.00–19.00hrs; Winter, daily, 10.00–18.00hrs.

◆
LOS HERVIDEROS
1 mile (2km) from El Golfo
The wild ocean pounds into sea-caves, at a point where boiling lava and Atlantic Ocean have met to create a tormented rockscape. The name means 'Boiling Springs'. There are stopping places for cars, with walkways down specially constructed steps at various vantage points offering views of the sea raging in the rocks.

◆◆◆
MIRADOR DEL RÍO
6 miles (9km) north of Haría
This breathtaking lookout point, set into the top of the high Riscar de Famara (Famara Cliff) on the extreme northerly point of the island, was built on the site of an earlier watch tower. The dreaded view then was of pirate ships on the horizon and in the 1898 Spanish-American war it was a gun battery. Now, from a height of 1,475 feet (450m) you see cliffs falling away sharply beneath to the Playa del Risco and the tiny multi-coloured squares of salt pans far below, the narrow strait of El Río and the island of Graciosa, edged by brilliant sandy beaches. The view to the west side of the island is of the Famara cliffs falling down to the coast below, the long stretch of Famara beach and the fishing village of Caleta. The *mirador* was designed by César Manrique with white curved walls, wooden floors, rocks, plants and nothing to distract you from the view.
Open: Summer, daily, 11.00–19.00hrs; Winter, daily 10.00–18.00hrs.

◆◆
MONUMENTO AL CAMPESINO
Mozaga, 5 miles (8km) northwest of Arrecife
This Monument to the Rural Worker, almost in the dead centre of the island, is a tribute by César Manrique to the skill and ingenuity of peasants who won back a living from the devastated earth. The sculpture itself is rather like a totem pole of white blocks, and at 50 feet (15m) high is visible from some distance. The Casa del Campesino beside it is an old farmhouse, now renovated and housing a museum of rural life through the ages. A courtyard restaurant serves local food and wine.
Open: daily, 10.00–18.00hrs.

◆◆◆
PARQUE NACIONAL DE TIMANFAYA ✓

entrance to park 4½ miles (7km) north of Yaiza
The volcanic eruptions that devastated the island in the 18th century created an extraordinary landscape, which has been a national park since 1974. It covers 20 square miles (50sq km). The highest crater is Timanfaya, 1,673 feet (510m). The park is now a national asset, but its creation was a national disaster. The parish priest at the village of Yaiza, Andrés Lorenzo Curbelo, described the first explosions in the evening of 1 September 1730 as a mountain rising out of the earth spewing flames which continued to blaze for 19 days. Those were the first days of volcanic activity which lasted for six years and buried 11 villages.

Montañas del Fuego

The 'Mountains of Fire' are the principal attraction of the national park. Entering from the village of Yaiza, the road passes through a level landscape of tormented black rock which then turns into a desert of loose black cinders. A horned devil holding a fork, the emblem of the park, stands on guard. In the distance the red and grey flanks of the craters rise out of the ground. Stop at the Echadero de los Camellos (Camel Park) and, amid the sometimes frenetic activity here, you can ride on a dromedary into the volcanic wasteland.

The conducted coach tour of the Mountains of Fire begins at the Islote de Hilario, once the 'desert island' of the hermit Hilario and now the central reception point of the park. The hermit in question apparently set up residence here after the eruptions were over, planting a miraculous fig tree on the spot. A withered tree, now incorporated into the Restaurante del Diablo, does indeed stand on this spot but its provenance is uncertain. To demonstrate the heat within the mountain – 750°F (400°C), an attendant pours water into a pipe inserted in the earth and beats a hasty retreat: five seconds later a great blast of steam whooshes out of the pipe. For a culinary demonstration at the restaurant, steaks are grilled over an open well. Beneath lies the natural furnace of the volcano an awe-inspiring and unlimited source of free heat. The **Ruta de los Volcánes coach tour** is a marvellous, theatrical and atmospheric experience of the volcanoes.

Open: daily, 09.00–17.00hrs.

Camel-riding side-saddle through the moonscape of Timanfaya

SALINAS DE JANUBIO

On the west coast, at the southern end of Timanfaya National Park, the Janubio Saltpans lie in the flat base of an old crater beside an enclosed lagoon. The sea water is pumped into the many rows of square pans and evaporated to leave little mounds of white salt. Lanzarote produces 10,000 tonnes a year, much of it for use in fish processing but some for table salt. Old broken down windmills are a reminder of former, less automated days of water-pumping.

TEGUISE

5½ miles (9km) north of Arrecife

The ancient former capital of the island was founded by Maciot de Béthencourt, nephew of Jean de Béthencourt, the original Norman conqueror of the Canaries. Despite repeated pirate attacks, the town has many fine old buildings.

The restored 15th-century church of San Miguel stands in the main square of the town. Facing it is the Renaissance façade of the Palacio de Spinola built in the 18th century by an Italian merchant, Vincente Spinola. It is restored and open to visitors. Other notable buildings include the 18th-century Convento de Santo Domingo and the 16th-century Convento de San Francisco, the latter in process of restoration. Teguise is the home of the *timple*, a Canarian stringed musical instrument, like a miniature guitar. You may have to look hard to find one because the tourist shops in the town stock only souvenirs of the most banal nature. On Sundays, there is a market in the square and displays of folk dancing and singing.

Outside the town but clearly visible from it is a castle, **Castillo de Guanapay**, or Castillo de Santa Bárbara. It stands on the rim of a crater, Montaña Guanapay, and was built in the 14th century by Lancelloti Malocello, the Genoese who probably gave the island his name.

TIMANFAYA see PARQUE NACIONAL DE TIMANFAYA

VILLA AGRÍCOLA EL PATIO
Tiagua (Sóo Road), 7½ miles (12km) northwest of Arrecife
Lanzarote's newest tourist attraction is a small group of old agricultural buildings, beautifully restored to illustrate life on the land between 50 and 100 years ago. An enthusiastic guide (speaking Spanish only) will show you into a windmill, a great barn converted to a museum, a *bodega* (wine store) and outhouses with various types of hand-powered mills and, to end the tour, you will be given a taste of local wine, cheese and breadsticks in an atmospheric bar area.

YAIZA
10 miles (16km) north of Playa Blanca
This village just south of the Timanfaya National Park is generally regarded as the prettiest on the island. It has some fine old houses and the 18th-century church of Los Remedios, a couple of good restaurants (including the famous La Era, see **Restaurants**) and a *casa de cultura* (cultural centre) showing the work of local artists. The gardens brim over with hibiscus and geraniums.
Galerie Yaiza open: daily, 17.00–19.00hrs.
closed: Sunday

Accommodation
Costa Teguise
Meliá Salinas, 5-star (tel: 59 00 40). Luxury hotel on beach, featuring a tropical hanging garden with pools and waterfalls and various sporting activities.

La Santa (near Tinajo)
Club La Santa (tel: 59 99 99). Famous as the 'No 1 sports resort in the world', it is the perfect place for sports and fitness enthusiasts with excellent

facilities, tuition and coaching.
Families are welcome and there
are excellent facilities for children,
plus the usual bars, restaurants,
shops, supermarkets, and discos.

Playa Blanca
Hotel Lanzarote Princess,
Costa Papagayo (tel: 51 71 08).
This spacious hotel has
bedrooms built around its
swimming pool area with views
out to sea. Ten minutes walk
from the main Playa Blanca
beach, it is cheerful and
comfortable, ideal for families.
Sports facilities include tennis,
volleyball and squash.

Puerto del Carmen
Riu Paraiso, 4-star, Playa de los
Pocillos (tel: 51 24 00).
Comfortable, with a large
swimming pool and sun terrace
area, bars, choice of restaurants,
gymnasium, live entertainment
and a friendly atmosphere.
Los Fariones, 4-star (tel: 51 01
75). Set just south of the Playa
Blanca beach and handy for the
harbour district. This is one of
the resort's older hotels and has
a beautiful mature garden of
palms of many kinds.
Recommended and not to be
confused with the same
company's new and over-large
apartment hotel, Los Fariones
Playa just next door.

Entertainment and Nightlife
In both Costa Teguise and Playa
Blanca, evening entertainment
programmes are usually
initiated by individual hotels.
They include cabaret acts,
flamenco dancers, competitions,
discos, all at varying levels
of professionalism.

The same goes for major hotels
in Puerto del Carmen but there
the choice is considerably
increased by clubs, pubs,
bars and discos in the harbour
and old town, as well as in
the arcades on the Avenida de
las Playas.
For bars with live music in
Puerto del Carmen, try
Amadeus, **Charlie's Bar** and
Diamond in the arcades along
the Avenida de las Playas. For
livelier action and noisier
music, try the **Waikiki Beach
Club** or **Rock Café**. **Paradise
Disco**, **Emporium-Havana
Club-Hippodrome**, **Dreams**
and **Moonlight Bay** nightclub
are all popular with the young.
Norah's tiny bar, **The
Dubliner**, in the old town, is
always crowded.

Restaurants
Arrecife
Castillo de San José (tel: 81 23
21). The walls of this restaurant
beneath the Museum of
Contemporary Art are hung
with pictures. The décor is
simple and elegant, the
views are stunning and the food
is excellent.

Costa Teguise
La Chimenea, Playa de las
Cucharas (tel: 81 47 00).
International cuisine in an
attractive beachside setting.
The service is excellent and this
is reflected in the prices.

Puerto del Carmen
El Sardinero, Plaza El Varadero
(tel: 51 19 33). A popular fish
restaurant on the harbour in the
old town. You can choose your
own fish – but the later you

leave it, the more likely you are to be left with just sardines. The décor is functional rather than elegant but the waiters are cheerful and so are the diners. **Candil**, on the Avenida de las Playas, is a lovely spot with good food and service. Steps decorated with black and white pebbles lead down to a beach-side terrace under palm trees. **O'Botafumeiro**, a Galician restaurant near the San Antonio Hotel towards Play de los Pocillos, serves delicious fresh seafood.

Teguise
Acatife is beautifully situated in the main square of Teguise. This restaurant serves both international and Canarian food. Try the excellent local dishes and drink the local wine. The meat is charcoal-grilled.

Yaiza
La Era (tel: 83 00 16). An attractive restaurant serving real Canarian food with verve and charm. Small dining-rooms are set round a floral courtyard. The old photographs on whitewashed walls, checked tablecloths and rush seat chairs give it a comfortable farmhouse look. The menu cover was designed by César Manrique. In a village full of flowers, the garden around this restaurant is positively choking with them.

Shopping
Most of the shops on the island are to be found in the **arcades** beside the Avenida de las Playas, Puerto del Carmen, and in the town itself. No great surprises. Some of the

embroidered cloth 'from the Canaries' has actually just come off the plane from Taiwan. Let the price be your guide.

Special Events
The February/March **Carnival** is a big event on the island, as is **Corpus Christi** in June. Instead of the carpets of flowers seen on the other islands, patterns of coloured sand are used to decorate the ground. In August everybody celebrates the feast of San Ginés, the patron saint of the island. Each town or village also celebrates its own saint's day. The **Fiesta de la Virgen de los Volcánes** on 15 September in the village of Mancha Blanca, district of Tinajo, marks a miraculous deliverance from the eruption of Las Quemadas volcano in 1824. The lava headed straight for Mancha Blanca. Terrified, villagers took their image of the Virgin to confront the molten flow, which was immediately diverted.

Sport
The best facilities on the island for most sports are to be found at the world-famous Club La Santa (see **Accommodation**). On Costa Teguise, there is an 18-hole **golf** course, about a mile (1.5km) from the hotel Meliá Las Salinas. Golf clubs can be hired. At Puerto del Carmen, the Insular Sports Club (near Los Fariones Hotel) has **swimming pool**, **tennis** and **squash courts**. The Castellana Sports Club specialises in **aerobics** and **weight training**. There are four **diving** schools at this resort.

PEACE AND QUIET

Wildlife and Countryside on the Canary Islands
by Paul Sterry

For many people, the Canary Islands conjure up images of blue skies, warm seas and sandy beaches, together with the usual tourist infrastructure of hotels and bars. However, there is another, far wilder side to the islands, and within a few miles of many of the tourist spots you can reach ancient lava flows, sulphurous volcanic cones and even snow-capped mountain tops with plants that would look equally at home in the Alps. The seven main islands vary from the semi-desert moonscape of the eastern isles, like Lanzarote, to the lush, humid western islands, like La Palma. The islands have been influenced by man for centuries, but despite a great deal of modern tourism and development, many areas have been set aside and protected. There are national parks on Lanzarote, Tenerife, La Gomera and La Palma, and 60 other nature reserves. The Canaries have an immense plant list, totalling nearly 2,000 species of flowering plant alone. Due to the early separation and isolation of the islands, many of the plants are found nowhere else in the world, an honour also shared by seven of the islands' bird species.

Lanzarote
Lanzarote is the easternmost island in the Canaries and together with Fuerteventura, is closest to the African mainland. Although not as mountainous as some of the other islands, the highest point being 2,214 feet (675m), the landscape is forbidding. The rugged hills and cliffs of Famara in the north are comparatively green compared to the plains and dunes of the south, while the southern and central countryside is volcanic, with craters and cinder deserts. Somehow the inhabitants still manage to grow crops.

Despite patchy development, the terrain is largely unspoilt and has rare and interesting birds. Houbara bustards (a globally endangered species) and black-bellied sandgrouse are typical desert species which find the hostile environment much to their liking.

For the botanist, the northern half of the island is undoubtedly the

The mighty Echium wildpretii *is an immense viper's bugloss which may be seen on Teide*

PEACE AND QUIET

Succulent Senecio kleinia *is well adapted to dry, salty conditions on Fuerteventura*

more rewarding, and especially the rugged Famara region. From the town of Haría you can explore the area and find a wide variety of endemic plants. The coastal cliffs support the fleabane *Pulicaria canariensis* and the daisy-like shrub *Astericus schultzii* with its pale yellow flowers, both of which are found here and on Fuerteventura, but nowhere else in the world. However, the dominant plants of the coast of Lanzarote are the succulent spurges (*Euphorbia* species) and stonecrop-like family of *Aeonium*.

The cliffs provide dramatic views and seascapes, and from the northernmost viewpoint, Mirador del Río, you can look north towards the islets of Graciosa, Montaña Clara and Alegranza, breeding sites for little shearwaters and Bulwer's petrels. The dashing Eleonora's falcon also breeds around the coast and its aerobatic skills make it easy to identify.

In the south of the island lies the Parc Nacional de Timanfaya, near the town of Yaiza. The park protects the most spectacular area of volcanic activity on the island with the highlight being the Montañas del Fuego. The whole area is scorched and utterly devastated; much of the scenery was created in a violent eruption in 1730. Because of the dangerous terrain, special tours and coaches are arranged to guide visitors to the best craters and lava flows, and individual sightseeing is discouraged.

Fuerteventura

Fuerteventura is very arid and barren. Most of the island is covered by rocky plains, although it does also have fine sandy beaches, particularly in the north and southeast.

The botanical interest of Fuerteventura is centred around the northern town of La Oliva and the southern peninsula of Jandía. On the northern coast by Corralejo great dunes are to be found; the plants that grow here face the same problems as coastal plants everywhere, namely the salt-laden air, the drying sea breezes and well-draining soil. Many of the plants are prostrate in form and include the colourful vetch *Lotus lancerottensis*, but succulents like *Senecio kleinia* are also common. Although the latter species is related to ragwort, its shrubby appearance makes it difficult to imagine anything less like the common European weed.

In the south of the island lies the rocky peninsula of Jandía, dominated by a volcanic ridge running down its spine. On either side of the ridge, the rock shelves into the sea and forms sandy beaches. In addition to the widespread succulents, several rare endemic plants are found along the coast including the spurge *Euphorbia handiensis*, while on the slopes above, the straggling viper's bugloss *Echium handiensis* can be found. This is the only place in the world where it grows.

Fuerteventura is a good island for the birdwatcher. Most of the species found here are adapted to a desert life and many, like the houbara bustard, cream-coloured courser and black-bellied sandgrouse are also widespread in north Africa. Fuerteventura is also host to two birds endemic to the Canary Islands. The Canary Island chat is like a pale version of the European stonechat; Berthelot's pipit is like a pale, grey meadow pipit. Both are probably descended from their more widespread relatives from Europe and isolation from the mainland has encouraged this process. Cultivated fields around the coast may sometimes attract these species but here you are more likely to find trumpeter finches, with their ridiculous trumpeting calls and stubby red beaks, and lesser short-toed larks. The pale, washed-out plumage of the larks gives them good camouflage as they feed along the furrows in the fields.

Gran Canaria

From Gran Canaria's central dome-like plateau, gorges and valleys radiate down to the sea and there are numerous volcanic cones which dot the landscape. Extraordinary succulent plants, like the endemic spurge *Euphorbia canariensis*, grow out of barren soil and rock and add to the scenic attraction of the landscape. With their swollen stems they could easily pass for cacti and resemble rows of organ pipes.

Because of the prevailing northeasterly trade winds, the north side of the island is more humid and was formerly cloaked by evergreen laurel forests. However, centuries of exploitation by man have reduced the forest to remnant woodlands such as those at Los Tilos near Moya. Although the woods are no longer extensive enough to support Bolle's pigeons or laurel pigeons, the

PEACE AND QUIET

ground vegetation is interesting, with Canary willow growing on the valley floor, while the slopes are covered with endemic laurels and holly.

In the centre of the island lies the plateau of Cruz de Tejeda which, although reaching an altitude in excess of 4,910 feet (1,500m), is still accessible by road. Berthelot's pipits are common near the summit and feed in the open ground. Their song is sometimes delivered in flight when they share the skies with plain swifts (plain is the species name) hawking for insects. The mountain flowers are also abundant on the plateau

Euphorbia canariensis *is at home in near-desert conditions*

with succulents like *Aeonium simsii* and the shrubby *Cheiranthus scoparius* – the latter a crucifer with delightful mauve flowers.

The forests of tall, slender Canary pines on Pinar de Tamadaba, in the northwest of Gran Canaria, are also well worth exploring. The rare and endemic blue chaffinch frequents the trees, together with great spotted woodpeckers and rock sparrows haunt open, rocky outcrops. Rock roses and asphodels are common in open areas under the pines and the abundant, shrubby, *Micromeria pineolens* adds a splash of colour with its pink flowers.

If you have time to spare, do not miss the Jardín Botánico in Tafira, near the capital. It holds examples of many of the endemic flowers, some of which are very difficult to find in the wild.

Tenerife

The main geological feature of Tenerife is the ridge of hills which runs down the spine of the island, dominated by the volcanic peak of Teide, highest mountain in the islands. From the ridge and peaks, ravines run down to the sea and to the north, steep cliffs are pounded by the sea; to the south the flat, coastal plain forms beaches. Seabirds can be seen from almost any promontory along the north coast. Early mornings and late evenings are best, especially when an onshore wind is blowing. Cory's and little shearwaters and the all-dark Bulwer's petrel are frequently seen, particularly during the hot summer months.

Tenerife's Spurges

The north coast of Tenerife is also extremely good for flowers, with the two main centres of interest being around Teno in the northwest and around Anaga in the northeast. The cliffs at Teno are dominated by succulent spurges, and many of these species of *Euphorbia* look more like cacti than European plants. This is not just a coincidence and there is a good reason for the similarity. Both *Euphorbia* species and cacti have evolved to cope with the same environmental pressures of heat, infrequent and low rainfall, and desiccation. The huge *Euphorbia canariensis* is common as is *Euphorbia balsamifera*, whose stems are much-branched and woody.

A loud call and red beak make the trumpeter finch unmistakable

In Anaga, in the northeast of the island, a ridge of hills rises to 3,360 feet (1,021m) and still holds the remnants of the once widespread evergreen laurel forest known locally as 'laurasilva'. The woods are particularly good at Monte de las Mercedes, near La Laguna, and the patient and lucky birdwatcher may occasionally catch sight of the Bolle's pigeon, a bird which is, sadly, fast approaching extinction, amongst the laurels. Canary holly grows among the laurels, and firecrests can be heard singing their high-pitched song from the tree canopy.

With careful searching, the keen botanist can locate endemic plants such as the shrubby *Bencomia caudata* and *Silene lagunensis* on the forested crags in the area.

Mount Teide

Tenerife is dominated by Mount Teide. Rising to 12,199 feet (3,718m) above sea level, it is not only the highest peak in the islands but also the highest mountain in Spanish territories. Often shrouded in mist and cloud on its north side and sometimes even capped with snow, the extinct volcano of Mount Teide lies in the centre of the island. Its scenery and wildlife interest is immense and it is now protected within the boundaries of the fascinating Parque Nacional del Teide. From the rim of the crater, known as Las Cañadas, you can get a wonderful view of the summit which can be reached by cable car or by foot, if you are feeling extremely energetic. Once at the top, the view is magnificent and on a clear day

you can see all the Canary
Islands stretching off into the
distance. In the skies around the
summit you may see plain swifts,
a small, dark species which is a
speciality of the Canaries and
Madeira, hawking for insects in
the updraughts. From the
Parador de las Cañadas you can
explore the surrounding scenery
and vegetation. It is dominated
by shrubby plants such as the
fragrant, white-flowered
Spartocytisus supranubius and
the sticky *Adenocarpus viscosus*
with its yellow, gorse-like
flowers. However, pride of place
must go to the immense and
majestic viper's bugloss, *Echium
wildpretii*. The dramatic scenery
of Mount Teide provides a
perfect setting for its huge spikes
of red flowers.

On the descent from the
parador, it is worth exploring
any area of Canary pine where
you may find canaries, ancestors
of the familiar, yellow cagebirds.

Blue Chaffinch
Pine forests are the haunt of the
blue chaffinch. These rare
birds, found only on the
Canaries, have a song which is
very similar to the common
chaffinch. However, blue
chaffinches are larger and the
males are a slaty-blue colour;
females are bluish but duller
than males. Their more familiar
relative, the chaffinch, is also
present on the Canaries but is
found at lower altitudes.

In open, rocky areas, you may
come across small parties of
barbary partridges, a species
widespread in north Africa.

*The lichen-draped laurel forests of
the Canaries have existed for
millions of years*

La Gomera
At the western extreme of the
Canary Islands lies the island of
La Gomera. Because of the
oceanic position, the humid
climate is quite unlike that of the
easterly islands and the peaks
are often shrouded in cloud.
Gomera is a tiny volcanic cone
with its summit almost in the
centre of the island. This peak
lies at the heart of the Parque
Nacional de Garajonay and from
the summit, valleys and ravines

neatly defined eyestripes and fiery crowns. They flit from branch to branch in the tree canopy above, while on the woodland floor the camouflaged markings of the woodcock make it difficult to spot. The ground vegetation of the evergreen forests is rich, with the St John's wort *Hypericum grandiflorum* and bushy figwort *Scrophularia langeana* being conspicuous. Further down the slopes where the leaf canopy opens out, tree heathers, rock roses and Canary broom add colour to the landscape.

El Hierro

A great part of the small island of El Hierro is inaccessible due to the sheer cliffs, which rise to a height of 4,900 feet (1,500m) at the island's summit. Its semi-circular shape suggests that it is probably part of an extinct volcano, but the slopes are now covered in dense evergreen laurel and pine woodland. The region known as El Golfo is one of the most accessible areas of laurel forest with a colourful woodland floor containing the cranesbill *Geranium canariense*. In open areas the giant spurge *Euphorbia regis-jubae* is common and reaches the height of some of the trees.

radiate down towards the sea. The clouds which often prevail on the peak's northern side have encouraged the development of evergreen forests and the humidity also favours the epiphytic lichens which festoon the branches of the trees. The forests of La Gomera hold the finest stands of laurel in the Canaries and provide some of the last few sites for two of the islands' rarest endemic birds. Both laurel and Bolle's pigeons occur here and are entirely dependent upon this habitat. The laurel woodlands also hold firecrests, resplendent with their

La Palma

La Palma still has extensive areas of forest, but the most impressive and best known feature of the island is its volcanic crater. The cone dominates the surrounding landscape, but for best effect it must be viewed from the rim. From the highest point, at nearly 8,000 feet (2,500m), you get a

PEACE AND QUIET

Adenocarpus viscosus *is unique to the Canary Islands*

panoramic view of the island and you can also look down into the crater itself, the Caldera de Taburiente, among the deepest volcanic craters in the world. The outer rim of the crater is heavily wooded and has a wide variety of shrubby legumes. The sticky *Adenocarpus viscosus* and bushy *Spartocytisus supranubius* are common here and are also found in the subalpine zone on Tenerife. These wild places are a favourite haunt of the aerobatic chough, its finger-like wing-tips in flight and loud 'chough' call making it easy to identify. On the ground it is a bit more ungainly as it probes for insects with its long, red bill.

The northeast region of La Palma is still heavily forested and remains the haunt of both laurel and Bolle's pigeons. From an elevated position you may see them flying over the forest canopy below and they can look superficially similar to a wood-pigeon. However, both species lack the woodpigeon's white wing patches and can be told from one another by the banded tail and speckled neck of the Bolle's pigeon.

In the southern tip of La Palma there is a vivid reminder that you are on a volcanic island. The volcano of Teneguía, near Fuencaliente, last erupted as recently as 1971, showering the surrounding land with ash.

The inhabitants of La Palma successfully manage to cultivate exotic crops like pineapple, avocado and banana in the uninviting soil and after the crops have been harvested, small flocks of birds gather to feed. Trumpeter finches and lesser short-toed larks are sometimes found on the ground, while spectacled warblers skulk in even the lowest bushy scrub around the field margins.

The Islands and their Flora: Origins and Future

The majority of the 2,000 or so species of flowering plants found on the Canaries are endemic to the islands. This is an amazing figure and is due in part to the great age of the islands and their lengthy isolation from the mainland of Africa.

Some of the Canaries' plants are widespread throughout the islands while others are distinctly local. The laurels and pines are now restricted to small pockets at high altitude on most of the islands, but were once more widespread on the northern sides of the western islands. Some plants, such as the tiny endemic violet, *Viola cheiranthifolia*, have probably never been widespread. This species has probably only ever occurred on the highest slopes of Mount Teide where it still grows today: its restricted distribution is due to its precise habitat needs. Sadly, other plants have not fared so well: the charming trailing vetch, *Lotus berthelotii*, is now almost unknown in the wild.

The origin of the islands themselves has obviously had a profound influence on the plants that are found there today. At one time, the island range was probably connected to Africa, gradually drifting away from the continent. Much of the archipelago's landscape has subsequently been affected by violent volcanic activity and some of the western islands are probably entirely volcanic in origin. The Canaries have probably been separated from the mainland since at least the Pliocene, a period in the earth's history, 15–20 million years ago,

The Dragon Tree

The biggest and most famous inhabitant of the islands is the dragon tree. A peculiarity of this tree is its lack of rings, which means that telling its age is very difficult. The largest and oldest tree, the Drago Milenario (at Icod de los Vinos, Tenerife), is between 500 and 3,000 years old. Guanches attributed magical properties to the tree and used its 'dragon's' blood' sap (which turns red in the air) to heal wounds.

This trailing vetch is one of the plants in the Canaries which is threatened by human activity

when the average global temperature dropped significantly. Evergreen laurel forests which once covered the entire Mediterranean and North African region died out throughout most of their range. However, they survived on the Canaries as the islands drifted away from the mainland because of the modifying influence of the ocean – turning the islands into living time capsules.

Sadly, since man's arrival, all but a few of the evergreen forests have been wiped out.

The Distribution of the Canary Flora and Man's Influence

The climate and geology of the Canaries have had a profound influence on the natural distribution of the plants of the islands as well as on the ability to grow crops. Both their oceanic position and the range of altitudes have encouraged a great diversity.

The islands are far from flat and the high altitudes of some have encouraged a series of natural plant 'zones' to develop, each with its own specially adapted plants. These range from the succulents around the coast through the evergreen laurels and pines to subalpine plants near the mountain summits. Man's influence has been most strongly felt around the coasts, but the forests have also suffered as trees were felled for timber and firewood.

Were it not for their oceanic position and prevailing trade winds, which moderate the extremes in temperature, the Canaries would have a Mediterranean-type climate with hot, dry summers and mild, wet winters. As it is, the moisture-laden northeasterly winds create almost permanent cloud-cover on the mountains, allowing evergreen trees to survive.

Low walls give crops shelter from the wind on Lanzarote

Agriculture

Over the years, the crops grown have reflected changing needs, so at one time the ice plant, *Mesembryanthemum crystallinum*, was grown for soda extraction. This was then replaced by prickly pears, new-world cacti, grown not for their own sake, but in order to feed the cochineal bugs which yielded cochineal dye. Nowadays, much of the Canaries' agriculture is geared to supplying market garden vegetables and fruit for export; tomatoes, potatoes and even bananas all thrive in the arid soil. The mild winters ensure that crops can be harvested earlier than in northern Europe and some are picked all year round.

Despite the volcanic soil, considerable success has been achieved in cultivating plants on the Canaries.
Considerable ingenuity has been necessary to get the most out of the harsh environment. There is little standing water so, instead, bore-holes in the mountainsides pipe it into reservoirs for irrigation. The wind is often harsh, especially the drying Saharan winds felt on Lanzarote. For protection, the plants are often grown in little hollows surrounded by lava and cinder walls and these also collect any rain that falls. As a result, vines and even fig trees are grown successfully.

Seabirds

The seas surrounding the Canary Islands are rich in marine life and large numbers of seabirds gather to feed on this bounty. Some of

Sabine's gull is one of the most elegant seabirds

them breed around the islands and are present for most of the year, while others are visitors from all over the world.
Seabirds are often seen from the islands themselves. Almost invariably, dawn and dusk are the best times of day, and an onshore breeze will certainly improve your chances for watching the birds. Boat trips and inter-island ferries provide the best opportunities for close-up views.
The most frequently seen species around the coast of the Canaries is Cory's shearwater. These large, brown birds fly with stiff wings, banking and gliding low over the water's surface. During strong winds, however, they often soar to great heights and make the best possible use of every gust and updraught. Cory's shearwaters are often joined by their diminutive relative, the little shearwater, which with its fluttering flight

PEACE AND QUIET

looks more like a puffin than a shearwater. Both little shearwaters and Bulwer's petrels (another speciality of the islands) breed on the offshore islets of Graciosa and Montaña Clara off Lanzarote.

During the later summer and autumn, the resident seabird numbers are swollen by migrant species. Great and sooty shearwaters are visitors from their south Atlantic breeding colonies, while from August onwards, Sabine's gulls become common. These most elegant of seabirds breed in the brief summers of the high Arctic, abandoning their breeding grounds before other species have finished nesting.

On any of the longer ferry trips you may see small, black seabirds with white rumps, following the boats. These are storm-petrels, and several different species occur in the waters off the Canaries. Madeiran storm-petrels breed on the Madeiran islands (to the north) and are found throughout the year. However, from May until October you can also find Wilson's storm-petrels, visitors from the Antarctic. Although the two species are superficially similar, Wilson's storm-petrels have longer legs and yellow feet with which they patter over the surface of the water.

Cochineal Bugs

Before the advent of modern synthetic chemicals, all dyes had natural origins and some of them came from most unlikely sources such as lichens, soil sediments and tree bark. However, there could have been no more peculiar a source than that for cochineal, which was the dried bodies of a special kind of bug. Cochineal is a dye which was, and to some extent still is, used to stain fibres red. Its source is the cochineal bug *Dactylopius coccus*, which thrives on prickly pear, and both of these were introduced to the Canaries from Mexico. The dye was so important to the economy of the islands that fields of the cactus were planted in order to support huge numbers of the bugs. Nowadays, a variety of synthetic dyes has largely replaced cochineal and the prickly pear fields have consequently fallen into disuse. However, these hardy cacti thrive on neglect and colonies of bugs, with their characteristic mealy appearance, can still be found on the islands.

Cochineal bugs on prickly pears may still be found near Guatiza, Lanzarote

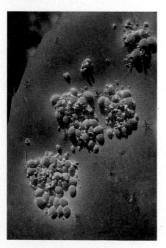

FOOD AND DRINK

There is a reasonable variety
of food and drink in the Canary
Islands, with most European
nations represented, including,
of course, Spain. The Canaries
also have many regional
specialities, all relying on
local produce. Some Canarian
favourites include:
Mojo sauce, used in *tipicos* (see
page 115) as an
accompaniment to fish and
meat dishes, is the most
distinctive element of Canarian
eating. Green mojo – *mojo
verde* – is based on parsley,
garlic and coriander. Red mojo
is based on sweet red pepper
but may be spiked with chilli. It
can be hot – taste cautiously
before applying. There are
many other mojo sauces, some
very complicated.
Sancocho is a rich fish stew,
generally of sea bass or salt cod,
poached with sweet potatoes
and served with mojo sauce.
Papas arrugadas – wrinkled
potatoes – are salty potatoes
boiled in their skins.
Rich soups full of bits and
pieces, amounting almost to
stew, are very popular.
Canarian *potaje* is a vegetable,
or meat-and-veg, first course
broth using local produce.
Canarians particularly enjoy
pork and rabbit. Fresh fish
is excellent.
Puddings are not to be missed.
If you can find it try *Bien me
sabe* – literally, 'How good it
tastes' – with real honey,
almonds and a dash of rum.
(When Canarians say *miel* –
honey in Spanish – they
generally mean cane syrup.)

*A café in Los Cristianos, Tenerife,
where it's always the season for
eating out of doors*

Another dessert worth seeking
out is *Frangollo*, made with *gofio*
(a roasted, powdered cereal
known to the ancient Guanche
inhabitants) and raisins, liberally
covered in 'honey'. Bananas are
cooked all kinds of ways, often
flambé, and *flan* – or caramel
pudding – is as popular as on
the Spanish mainland.

Drink
Local wines are found
throughout the islands, though
quality varies. Lanzarote's
speciality is *Malvasia*, or
Malmsey. **Water** – drink bottled
where possible.

SHOPPING

The Canary Islands have long enjoyed free port status. Though not always competitive, they are worth considering for the kind of articles normally found in duty free shops at airports, and for electronic goods. There is also attractive local produce on the larger islands. Suggestions are given for each island individually.

ACCOMMODATION

The major resorts have many large hotels, generally modern and comfortable, with all the facilities that might be expected in seaside resorts – swimming pools, basic sports facilities, evening entertainment … and so on. Most resorts, have numerous apartment hotels or 'aparthotels'. These are similar to regular hotels (with facilities like full dining-room service) but also have small kitchens for each room or suite, and probably a food shop on the premises as well. The smaller islands have smaller hotels. Five of the islands also offer *parador* hotels. These belong to Spain's excellent state-run chain, usually in interesting, sometimes isolated positions and occupying characterful buildings, old or new. There are few *pensions* in the Canaries; small inland towns and fishing villages are the best places to search these out. On the larger islands, villas are available through tour operators. They are generally well fitted out. In recent years, time-share apartments have been increasing in number. They have often been aggressively marketed and time-share touts are a nuisance on Tenerife and Gran Canaria. If you view time-share properties do so with great caution and sign nothing without seeking legal advice.

The palm garden and pool of the Los Fariones 4-star hotel, Puerto del Carmen, Lanzarote

CULTURE, ENTERTAINMENT AND NIGHTLIFE

Nightlife in the larger resorts is centred around discothèques, bars and casinos. For something traditionally Canarian, however, there are folklore shows, fiestas and the *Carnaval*. (For further details see each island entry in the **What to See** section.)

WEATHER AND WHEN TO GO

For most European countries, particularly Scandinavia and Germany, the 'season' for the Canaries is winter. It is generally warm enough to swim and to get a good sun-tan. The British tend to visit the Canaries all year round. A word of warning, though, to accompany the favourable sunshine statistics. The northern sides of almost all the islands are rainier than the south – because this is where the cloud-forming, moisture-bearing trade winds first make contact. Northern resorts

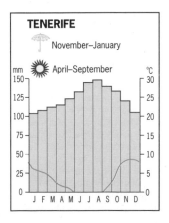

TENERIFE

☂ November–January

☀ April–September

mm													°C
150													30
125													25
100													20
75													15
50													10
25													5
0	J	F	M	A	M	J	J	A	S	O	N	D	0

can be quite wet and the whole of an island may be overcast for days in a row. Winds can be strong the whole year round. This being said, the climate is on the whole admirable, and claims of a year-round springtime are by no means far-fetched.

HOW TO BE A LOCAL

If you want to see real Canarians at play, just walk into any busy café, buy a coffee or a beer and take a ringside seat. Cafés are usually fairly spartan, noisy recreational meeting areas, male-oriented (though women do go there, too) and tolerant of children any time of day and night. When it comes to breakfast, order *tostado* (toast) or *donuts* (self-explanatory) washed down with *café solo* (espresso) or, if you can't take it harsh and black early in the morning, a drop of milk will turn it into a *cortado* (only tourists order *café con leche*!). Around midday those tasty Spanish snacks, *tapas*, are unveiled. This may be anything from the humble *tortilla* (potato omelet) to small fishes, beans, stews of all kinds and the ubiquitous salami-style sausages and cheese. For a more formal meal go to a *típico*, a no-nonsense restaurant (often rustic) where the food is more prized than the décor and where Sunday family gatherings have the air of a mini fiesta. English and German are widely spoken on the larger islands but elsewhere a few words of Spanish will go a long way. Do respect local communities, particularly in rural parts, by dressing conservatively when visiting churches.

Carnival at Las Palmas

CHILDREN

The Canaries offer a lot for children in terms of climate and general facilities. For particular venues, see individual islands.

TIGHT BUDGET

• A significant saving can often be made by booking holidays at the very last minute.
• You rarely have to pay an entrance fee to get into a disco.
• The 'menu of the day' often works out cheaper than snacks.
• Choose local beer rather than imported brands.
• The Tenerife and Gran Canaria bus services are cheap and reliable.
• Use public call boxes – much cheaper than hotel phones.
• It makes sense to shop where the locals shop. Most items are cheaper in ordinary shops than at the airport duty-free shop.

• La Gomera, La Palma and El Hierro are beautiful and there's little need to use your wallet.

SPECIAL EVENTS

Carnival is a major event usually in late February or early March. So, in several islands, is Corpus Christi in June. For events, see individual islands.

SPORT

There is plenty to choose from; some pointers are given under individual island entries. There are also some homegrown sports, notably the very popular Canarian wrestling, *lucha Canaria*, deriving directly from the original Guanche inhabitants. This is a gentlemanly team affair requiring agility and balance rather than brute strength. Newspapers give venues. There is another Guanche survival, the *Juego del Palo* or 'stick game', a kind of quarter-stave combat akin to fencing.

DIRECTORY

Arriving
By Air
Tenerife, Gran Canaria (Las Palmas), Lanzarote and Fuerteventura have international airports and all the islands can be reached on inter-island flights.

The airport on Gran Canaria is named Gando, 12½ miles (20km) south of Las Palmas. The airport bus to Las Palmas leaves every 30 minutes. A public bus service to the city runs every 15 minutes. Tenerife has two airports, the large and modern Reina Sofia (Tenerife Sur)airport in the south, already needing expansion, and Los Rodeos (Tenerife Norte) in the north, now used mainly for inter-island flights. In 1977, Los Rodeos was the scene of a disaster, caused by the collision of two jumbo jets; this and the rapid growth of tourism lay behind the decision to build a new airport in the south. Here there is a better approach and generally better weather conditions. There are no special problems associated with the other airports.

By Sea
The islands can be reached by regular services from Cádiz on the Spanish mainland to Santa Cruz (Tenerife), Las Palmas (Gran Canaria) and Arrecife (Lanzarote), so those coming for long periods can bring their own vehicles, but be prepared for a two-day voyage. Consult the Spanish Tourist Office for details of services.

Camping
Only Tenerife and Gran Canaria have official camp sites but nobody objects if the odd tent goes up. However, you cannot camp in a national park.

Chemist see Pharmacist

Crime
In the smaller islands there is little cause for concern but in cities like Las Palmas it is advisable to keep an eye on your belongings and your person, at certain times and in certain places.

Theft from cars is the most common form of crime against

tourists on the islands. Always remember to keep your car locked and never leave anything of value inside, even locked in the boot. Most hotels have safe deposit facilities which you would do well to use.

Customs Regulations

There are no limits on the amounts of alcohol and tobacco that can be brought onto the islands, but the prices of these products are so low in the Canaries that it seems a pointless exercise. Despite the Canaries' EU status the restricted export duty-free limits on drinks, tobacco, perfumes etc are still in force: 200 cigarettes or 100 cigarillos or 250g tobacco or 50 cigars; 1 litre of spirits over 22° proof or 2 litres fortified or sparkling wine, plus 2 litres of still wine; 60cc perfume or 250cc toilet water; £32 worth of gifts per person, but not more than 50 litres of beer or 25 cigarette lighters.

Driving
● Car Hire

All valid British, European, American and Australian licences are acceptable. There are plenty of car hire firms on all the islands, usually with unlimited mileage. Prices vary considerably between large hire companies and small local firms: shop around, keeping in mind that this may reflect genuinely competitive rates or hazardous corner-cutting in maintenance. In the event of breakdown or accident, telephone the local

Vilaflor, one of the picturesque villages of Tenerife

office of your car hire firm and be sure to follow the instructions given in your rental documentation.
The same rules apply as in Spain and the rest of mainland Europe – drive on the right, overtake on the left and give way to traffic approaching from the right unless there are contrary signs.
Use of seat belts is compulsory. Children under 10 must travel in the back of the car.
In towns, cars must be parked facing the same direction as movement of traffic.

• Speed Limits
Motorways 120kph (74mph);
roads with two or more lanes in
each direction 90kph (56mph);
built-up areas 60kph (37mph).

Electricity
The current throughout the
islands is 220 volts AC and
sockets take the circular two-
pin continental-style plug. If you
are really out in the wilds you
may find 110 volts supply, but
this is rare. Power cuts are not
infrequent, so pack a torch.

Embassies and Consulates
Gran Canaria
United Kingdom: P O Box
20202, Edificio Cataluña, Calle
Luis Morote, 6, Las Palmas,
35080 (tel: 26 25 08)

Tenerife
United Kingdom: Plaza Weyler
8, Santa Cruz de Tenerife,
38003 (tel: 28 68 63/28 66 53).
Irish Republic consulate:
Calle de Castillo 8, Santa
Cruz de Tenerife (tel: 24 56
71/24 50 35).

Emergency Telephone Numbers
In the event of a medical or
personal accident emergency
consult your hotel reception or
directory enquiries for your
local ambulance or red cross
(*cruz roja*) number. For an
emergency which requires the
attention of the police tel: 091
(all islands).

Entertainment Information
Details of events, festivals and
other entertainments can be
found in local newspapers and
magazines (see **Media**).

• Documents
Most visitors to the Canaries
use hire cars. For those who
plan a longer stay and wish to
take their own car, you would
be well advised to consult the
Spanish Tourist Office or
motoring associations.

• Petrol
Petrol is expensive and it's
best to carry cash, as the
majority of petrol stations do
not accept credit cards. These
are relatively numerous along
the main roads with 24-hour
opening in the larger resorts
and towns. Don't drive into the
mountains on an empty tank
however. There are few, if any,
filling stations and those steep
winding roads are very thirsty.

DIRECTORY

Entry Formalities

A valid passport, but no visa, is required by citizens of the EU, the US, Canada, Australia and New Zealand for stays of up to three months. To extend your stay, apply to police authorities. No paid work is allowed during this time.

Health Regulations

No special vaccinations are required.

Health Care

Similar to mainland Spain. Standards are generally acceptable. Most doctors speak and understand some English. Citizens of EU states are eligible for free medical and hospital

Intricate embroidery is a local speciality

treatment and pay only for dental treatment and prescribed medicines. (This involves obtaining Form E111 for UK travellers, before leaving home; if needed, it should be presented to the local office of the Instituto de la Seguridad Social.) Short-stay visitors should also take out some form of independent insurance cover. Non-EU nationals should always take out private insurance.

Holidays

Fixed Dates

1 January – Año Nuevo (New Year's Day)
6 January – Los Reyes (Epiphany)
2 February – La Candelaria (Candlemass)
19 March – San José (St Joseph's Day)
1 May – Día del Trabajo (Labour Day)
25 July – Santiago (St James's Day)
15 August – Asunción (Assumption)
12 October – Día de la Hispanidad (Discovery of America, Columbus Day)
1 November – Todos los Santos (All Saints)
6 December – Día de la Constitución (Constitution Day)
8 December – Immaculáda Concepción (Immaculate Conception)
25 December – Navidad (Christmas)

Movable Feasts

Jueves Santo (Maundy Thursday)
Viernes Santo (Good Friday)
Pascua (Easter Sunday)
Lunes de Pascua (Easter Monday)
Corpus Christi (May/June)

Lost Property

Report details to Municipal Police or *Guardia Civil* (see **Police** for phone numbers).

Media

There are several newspapers and magazines written for the English-speaking visitor to the Canary Islands. Gran Canaria has surprisingly few. Lanzarote has *Lanzarote Holiday Gazette* (free) and *Lancelot*, available from newsagents. On Tenerife look out for the newspaper *Island Connections* and the monthly magazine *Island Gazette* in the newsagents plus the free magazine *Tenerife Holiday Gazette*. La Palma has an annual magazine guide, *Guía Practica*. Free magazines are available from tourist offices, travel agents, hotels and popular bars.

All the major international papers are available in the large towns and popular resorts the day after publication, though the *International Herald Tribune* and *The Guardian* (international edition) can arrive the same day. Radio Canarias-Sol provides news and tourist information in English (Monday to Friday 08.00–08.30hrs, 15.00–15.30hrs, 16.30–17.00hrs) and German at most other times on 99.6 FM. Radio Maspalomas also provides a German language magazine programme from Sunday to Friday 18.00–20.00hrs on 95.3 FM. On Tenerife, Canary Island Tourist Radio broadcasts in English from Monday to Saturday on 747 MW.

Money Matters

In January 2002 euro banknotes and coins will come into circulation with a value of 166.39 pesatas to 1 euro and for a short time a dual pricing system will operate. On 28 February 2002 pesatas will be withdrawn from use. Banks are open weekdays 09.00–14.00hrs, Saturdays 09.00–13.00hrs, closed Sundays. All banks accept major credit cards – American Express, Diners Club, Access, Eurocard, Visa. You can change money at banks, exchange offices and larger hotels. The commission varies but is often hefty. Even if the rates on display seem attractive, the deductions which they fail to advertise will cost you dearly.

Credit Cards

Larger hotels, classier restaurants, banks, major shops and car rental firms will accept all major credit cards. Petrol stations normally will not.

Opening Times

Offices

Usually Monday to Friday 09.00–13.00hrs and 15.00–19.00hrs; Saturday 09.00–13.00hrs.

Shops

Usually 09.00–13.00hrs and 16.00–20.00hrs; Saturday 09.00–13.00hrs. But this may vary. For museum opening times, consult individual entries.

Personal Safety

Children particularly should be protected from sunburn. Always take water, extra clothing and wear stout shoes or boots on any expedition at high altitude, for instance on Mount Teide in Tenerife, or where the weather is likely to be changeable.

Pharmacist

Open: normal shopping hours Monday to Friday 09.00–

13.00hrs, 16.00–20.00hrs; Saturday 09.00–13.00hrs. Identified by the word **Farmacia** and a green cross shop sign. Each pharmacy should display the address of the nearest duty pharmacy or **Farmacia de Guardia** open outside these hours. After 22.00hrs only medicines on prescription are issued. Some medicines requiring a prescription in other countries are sold across the counter in Spain. Shops called *droguerias* sell cosmetics, not drugs or medicines.

Places of Worship

Spanish churches are normally Roman Catholic. Visitors are very welcome to attend their services.

Church of England services are held at All Saints Church, Taoro Park, Puerto de la Cruz, Tenerife (vicar, tel: 38 40 38), and Holy Trinity Church, corner of Calle Brasil and Calle Rafael Ramirez, Las Palmas, Gran Canaria (chaplain's residence, tel: 25 72 02). The Templo Ecuménico near the Kasbah precinct, Playa del Inglés, holds services for different denominations in turn.

Police

There are three different police forces. The **Policía Municipal** (Municipal Police) in blue uniform and cap, have responsibility for traffic. The **Policía Nacional** wear brown and berets and are in charge of crime control. The **Guardia Civil** (Civil Guard) in pea-green uniform and cap or sometimes in distinctive black patent leather tricorn hat, are responsible for coasts and customs, rural areas and highway patrol.

The emergency number which can be dialled to reach police in all islands is: 091.

Post Office

Post and Telegraph offices (**Correos y Telégrafos**) open Monday to Friday 09.00–14.00hrs; Saturday 09.00–13.00hrs. You cannot telephone from a post office but you can send a telegram – or dictate one by telephone, tel: 22 20 00. See also **Telephones**. Spanish post boxes are yellow. All mail leaves the Canaries by air and takes at least 5 days to reach northern European addresses. Stamps are available at most tobacconists and shops selling post cards as well as at post offices.

Public Transport
● Air

All islands have an airport and are connected by inter-island flights. Flights between Tenerife and Gran Canaria are almost hourly. Inter-island flights are well used by islanders; early booking is advisable.

● Ferries

All islands can be reached by ferries, mostly run by the Compañía Trasmediterránea. There is an additional jetfoil/hydrofoil service between Las Palmas (Gran Canaria) and Santa Cruz (Tenerife) and from both to Morro Jable (Fuerteventura). La Gomera is reached by ferry or hydrofoil from Los Cristianos on Tenerife (35 minutes by hydrofoil).

● Buses

Buses are a good way of getting about on Tenerife and Gran Canaria where the services are frequent and reliable. The smaller islands are rather less

Playa Calera is one of La Gomera's few beaches. It lies at the end of Valle Gran Rey

well served. Multi-journey tickets give a 40 per cent discount on fares and can be bought at TITSA (bus operator) offices or some banks.

- **Taxis**
Identified by the letters SP on the front and rear of a car, standing for 'servicio público'. Most are metered at a rate fixed by the municipal authorities. There are usually fixed rates for long distances. Confirm the fare before beginning the journey.

Senior Citizens

The winter climate of the Canaries is ideal for, and much enjoyed by, senior citizens. Facilities are generally modern and standards of comfort high.

Student and Youth Travel

There are no youth hostels in the Canaries.

Telephones

Each province has its own code: **922** for Tenerife, La Gomera, El Hierro and La Palma; **928** for Gran Canaria, Lanzarote and Fuerteventura. When calling from one province to another, use the full code and then dial the number required. When calling inside a province simply dial the number, not the code.

Codes to the Canaries

Dial 00–34, then the provincial code, omitting the initial 9. For the province of Tenerife dial 00–34–22 then the number; for Gran Canaria, Lanzarote and Fuerteventura, dial 00–34–28 then the number.

Codes from the Canaries

Dial the country code (UK 07–44; Eire 07–353; US and Canada 07–1; Australia 07–61; New Zealand 07–64); then the local code, omitting the initial zero; then the number.

Public Telephones

Instructions show you how to place your coins in the machine so that they roll down as needed. Dialling as above.

Time (local)

The Canaries maintain Greenwich Mean Time in the winter, which is one hour behind most European countries and in line with the UK. The clocks go back one hour in summer. The Canaries are five hours ahead of US Eastern Standard Time, and eight hours ahead of Pacific Time. Johannesburg is ahead by one hour, Australia by 10 hours and New Zealand by 12 hours.
Note that there are two brief periods of a one-hour difference (in late September and late March) owing to different start/end dates to summertime.

Tipping

Most bills have service charge included but it is customary to leave an extra 5 per cent or so, or at least the small change.

Toilets

Public toilets are rare. The wise remember to use the facilities in the restaurants and bars they patronise. If you are desperate, no barman will mind if you pop in and ask to use the toilet.

Tourist Offices
United Kingdom

Spanish National Tourist Office, 23 Manchester Square, London W1M 5AP (tel: 020 7 486 8077).

US

Spanish National Tourist Office, 666 Fifth Avenue, New York, NY 100103 (tel: 212 265 8822).

Canada

Spanish National Tourist Office, 2 Bloor Street West, 34th floor, Toronto, Ontario M4W 3E2 (tel: 416 961 3131).

Tenerife

Playa de las Américas Playa de Troya, Avda Litoral (tel: 79 76 68). **Puerto de la Cruz** Plaza de la Iglesia 3 (tel: 38 60 00). **Santa Cruz** Palacio Insular, Plaza de España (tel: 60 55 92).

La Gomera

Calle del Medio, San Sebastián (tel: 14 01 47).

El Hierro

Licenciado Bueno, 3 Valverde (tel: 55 03 02).

La Palma

Calle O'Daly 6, Santa Cruz (tel: 41 21 06).

Gran Canaria

Las Palmas Casa del Turismo, Parque de Santa Catalina (tel: 26 46 23) and Pueblo Canario (tel: 24 35 93).

Fuerteventura

Cabildo Insular, 1° de Mayo, 33 Puerto del Rosario (tel: 85 10 24).

Lanzarote

Parque Municipal, Arrecife (tel: 81 18 60) and Avda Marítima de las Playas, Puerto del Carmen (tel: 51 33 51).

LANGUAGE

yes sí
no no
please por favor
thank you gracias
good morning buenos días
good night buenas noches
I want quiero
I am looking for busco
where is? ¿dónde está?
how much? ¿cuánto es?
airport aeropuerto
beach playa
hotel hotel
restaurant restaurante
beer cerveza
milk leche
water agua
wine vino
bread pan
fish pescado
fruit fruta
meat carne
pudding postre

can I have? ¿me da?
chemist una farmacia
doctor el médico
expensive caro
help ayuda
hospital hospital
I've lost my... he perdido mi...
luggage equipaje
map un mapa
market un mercado
mineral water agua mineral
name el nombre
newspaper un periódico
night noche
number número
pardon? ¿cómo?
passport pasaporte
police la policía
postcard una postal
stamp un sello
room la habitación
shower ducha
suitcase una maleta

La Palma's volcanic crater

INDEX/ACKNOWLEDGEMENTS

Acknowledgements

The Automobile Association would like to thank the following photographers and libraries for their assistance in the compilation of this book:

J ALLAN CASH PHOTO LIBRARY 5 Windmill, 8 Farming nr. Agaete, 9 Teide's crater, 14 Los Gigantes, 19 Candelaria, 29 Flower market, Santa Cruz, 31 Gomera, Valle Gran Rey, 37 Vallehermoso, 39 El Golfo, 42/3 Roques de Salmór, 45 Santa Cruz, 48 Ayuntamiento, Santa Cruz, 50/1 San Antonio, Fuencaliente, 55 Caldera de Taburiente, 66 Doramas Park, Las Palmas, 68/9 View from Cruz de Tejeda, 74 Folk Dancing, 76 Golfing, 77 Windmill, Fuerteventura, 80 Fuerteventura, 83 Pájara, 93 Arrecife, 94 Towards Haría, 97 Camel rides, 113 Los Cristianos, 116 Carnival, 120 Embroidery, 123 Playa Calera, 125 La Palma's crater.
A HOPKINS 20 Dragon Tree, 35 El Cercado, 36 Valle Gran Rey, 85 Windsurfing, 114 Palm Garden.
GABRIELLE MACPHEDRAN 41 The Ermita of La Dehesa.
INTERNATIONAL PHOTOBANK Cover Lido Martiánez, Tenerife, 18 Santa Cruz, 22 Valle de la Orotava, 24/5 Caldera de Las Cañadas, 62 Maspalomas, 118/9 Vilaflor.
NATURE PHOTOGRAPHERS LTD 101 Wildpretii (B Burbidge), 102 Senecio kleinia (K J Carlson), 104 Euphorbia canariensis (B Burbidge), 105 Trumpeter finch (R Tidman), 106/7 Laurel forest (B Burbidge), 108 Adenocarpus viscosus (B Burbidge), 109 Trailing vetch (B Burbidge), 110 Fig Tree (N A Callow), 111 Sabine's gull (D Goodfellow), 112 Cochineal bug (S C Bisserot).
The remaining photographs are held in the Association's own photo library (© AA PHOTO LIBRARY) and were taken by Clive Sawyer.

Contributors for this revision:
Verifier: Paul Murphy; Copy editor: Sheila Hawkins